# Introduc
# to software
# design

# Introduction to software design

## Stephen Heaven MSc, BSc

Natural Environment Research Council
*Formerly* Lecturer in Computer Systems, Brunel College of Arts & Technology

Edward Arnold
A member of the Hodder Headline Group
LONDON  MELBOURNE  AUCKLAND

First published in Great Britain 1995 by
Edward Arnold, a division of Hodder Headline PLC,
338 Euston Road, London NW1 3BH

*British Library Cataloguing in Publication Data*
A catalogue record for this book is available from the British Library

ISBN 0-340-59458-6

1  2  3  4  5     95  96  97  98  99

Produced by Gray Publishing, Tunbridge Wells, Kent
Printed in Great Britain by The Bath Press, Avon

# Contents

# Preface

Computer software is now widely used in all branches of engineering. It is becoming increasingly important for today's engineering technicians to have some knowledge of software design. This book is intended to cover most of the work in the BTEC unit Software Design Methods at level N.

The intention is to introduce the student to the concepts of software design and implementation. C and Pascal are used for examples of how designs may be implemented in a block structured language. It is not intended as a text on programming in either C or Pascal. In particular it does not cover all the features or nuances of either language. But is intended to show how to design well-structured programs. A book is no substitute for practical work, and most is learned from designing, writing, compiling and testing programs.

I would like to take this opportunity to thank my former colleagues at Brunel College of Arts & Technology, Don Davidson and Nigel Furness, for their help in developing the course upon which this book is based. I would also like to thank Dr Russell Parry and the staff at Edward Arnold for their guidance and support.

## ACKNOWLEDGEMENTS

Figure 3.7 By kind permission of Clarion (Europe) Ltd.

Figure 3.8 By kind permission of Borland International.

# 1 Why software design?

Software controlled products are now in widespread use in everyday life. Advances in microelectronic technology mean that often the most cost-effective way of producing a product is to use a general-purpose microprocessor. The features of the product are then supplied by programming the microprocessor. This means that often the only substantial difference between two products is the software. Engineering is becoming increasingly dependent on software.

Traditional engineering disciplines such as civil, mechanical and electrical engineering have over many years developed their own accepted procedures and practices. These have evolved to enable practising engineers to produce good, reliable products. Software engineering is a relatively new discipline, and has evolved very quickly. In the past there has been a tendency for software implementation to move ahead of the development of sound engineering practices. With the increasing reliance on software it is even more important that sound engineering practice is applied to the design and production of software.

## SOFTWARE LIFE CYCLE

The whole process associated with the production of a piece of software is known as the software life cycle. Various models of the life cycle have been produced; Fig. 1.1 shows a simplified model.

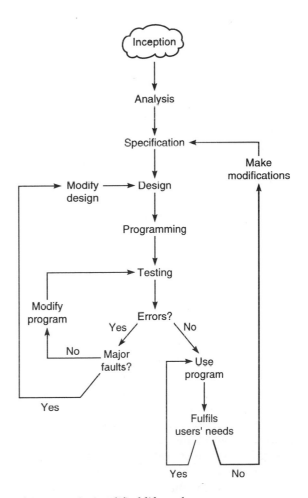

**Figure 1.1** A simplified life cycle.

From the model it is possible to identify four phases.

- Definition
- Design
- Implementation
- Maintenance.

This book is concerned mainly with design, implementation and some aspects of maintenance. We will not concern ourselves with the definition phase.

# THE DESIGN PHASE

In branches of engineering such as mechanical, electronic and civil engineering, design is accepted as an essential part of the manufacturing process. A car, a television or a bridge are not simply constructed from the raw materials. A great deal of thought and effort is spent on designing the product before any construction takes place. Unfortunately this has not always the case with software. Programmers are sometimes tempted to produce a software solution to an engineering problem "off of the top of their head". The process of designing and coding the program at the keyboard is analogous to giving a civil engineer a pile of girders with some nuts and bolts and saying "build a bridge". It is just possible that a bridge will emerge, but would you trust it?

Because of the ease with which software can be put together, tested, changed and re-tested this unstructured, trial-and-error approach can seem to work. An apparently working product can be produced quite quickly. However, software produced this way can never be fully trusted and is usually a source of problems for the future.

Following a formal, structured design method does not not guarantee a good design, nor a good product, but it does lessen the chances of a bad design. How can we judge what is a good design and what is a bad design? We must establish some criteria against which we can assess our designs. Academics in the field have suggested mathematical methods by which software designs may be measured. But at this introductory level we will be content to establish some aims which will be our goal.

## Design aims

A car manufacturer setting out to design a new model will have certain aims. This may include the desirable attributes of:

- Low fuel consumption
- Aesthetic style
- Ease of manufacture
- Performance
- Reliability, and so on.

These may not all be achievable in one design, but they are design aims.

Experience has shown that the following are desirable for a piece of software so we shall make them our aim

- Reliability
- Maintainability
- Performance
- Portability.

## Reliability

A reliable piece of software is one which, given the same set of conditions, will always produce the same results. This repeatability of results is essential. If the software sometimes produces one result, and sometimes another, how do we know which is correct? A piece of software which, under certain circumstances, is always wrong is more reliable than another piece of software which is sometimes right.

Software reliability is its capacity to act consistently time and time again.

## Maintainability

All engineering products need to be maintained. However, unlike mechanical or electronic products, software does not suffer from wear and tear.

The term "software maintenance" is used to refer to all the work carried out after the program has started to be used. Maintenance falls into three categories:

❏ *Corrective maintenance.* This covers the work involved in correcting errors or "bugs" discovered in the program by the users. These may be due to incorrect implementation or incorrect design.
❏ *Adaptive maintenance.* During its lifetime a program may need to be adapted to a changed environment. Any modifications required to transfer a program from one computer system to another come under this category. A program may also need to be modified if the system on which it runs is upgraded. Maintenance under this category does not include any changes or enhancements to the functionality of the program.
❏ *Perfective maintenance.* As a result of the experience of users, programs are often upgraded or enhanced. This may mean performing the same function but better, e.g. faster. Or the functionality of the software may be increased as in an upgrade. Improving the performance or upgrading of software is perfective maintenance.

## Performance

By performance we do not mean that the software merely meets the specification, but it does so using the minimum of the computer's resources. Processor time and memory space are both finite resources on any computer system. A program which fulfils its specification using a minimum of these two resources is a desirable aim.

## Portability

The computer industry is beset with the problem of incompatibility. Hardware peripherals for one computer may not work with a different computer, and software for one computer may not run on another. A portable program is one which can be successfully transferred from one type of computer to another with little or no modification. If programs are designed in a modular form then the neces-

sary changes can be confined to just one module. A program designed to be portable will be less difficult to maintain in the future.

Ideally one design will maximize all of the above aims. However, in practice there has to be some trade-off between competing aims. For example, performance, in terms of speed of operation, can often be increased by making use of the special facilities of a particular computer. But this is at the expense of portability.

Adopting a modular approach to design has great benefits, particularly in the areas of maintenance and reliability. Using this approach the software is divided into a set of smaller modules, each of which can be specified and designed separately.

Well-designed modules are:

■ *Simple*: Easy to build, easy to maintain, easy to test.
■ *Reliable*: A simple module is easier to program correctly, so it is more likely to be error free.
■ *Reusable*: Savings can be made on redundant programming effort by building reusable modules (avoid reinventing the wheel). A module previously tested and known to be working improves reliability.

## THE IMPLEMENTATION PHASE

The implementation of a software solution is the process of transferring a design to a program. This stage, sometimes referred to simply as programming, appears to the novice to be the most productive. The act of writing a program is seen as creative, in fact the most creative stage is the design phase. Most engineers new to software spend the majority of their time in programming. Time spent on the design phase is repaid several times over at the implementation phase.

A modular design should be implemented as a modular program. Modern programming languages are inherently modular in structure, though a program written in an unstructured language can still be modular.

Some of the advantages of modular programs are:

- A single module is easier to write and test than a whole program.
- Modular programming allows for the re-use of previously written modules.
- The effect of errors can often be confined to a single module.
- Upgrades may be possible by changes to one module rather than the whole program.
- By dividing up the task logically more than one programmer may work on the program at the same time.

## Disadvantages of modular design

There are some drawbacks to designing in a modular fashion, rather than a linear, mono-lithic approach. In general the disadvantages are far outweighed by the advantages, but there may be special circumstances where a modular design is not the best approach.

### Disadvantages

Integrating the modules together may prove a complex and time-consuming task.

Modular programs often require more memory and more processing time than non-modular programs.

To test individual modules extra software has to be written to provide the interface to the module under test. This obviously requires extra effort. Also the test driver software may, itself, introduce errors.

## THE MAINTENANCE PHASE

The working life of a program may span several years. During this time the program must be supported. There may be changes, due to newly discovered errors or enhancements, to be made. It is most unlikely that the original programmer will still be available to carry out these duties. Studies have shown that up to 50 percent of programmers' time can be spent working on programs they did not originate. Here again a clear, modular design and a modular program are of benefit.

## SUMMARY

- ❏ The software life cycle consists of definition, design and implementation and maintenance.

- ❏ In order to achieve desired aims, software must be properly designed.

- ❏ A modular approach to design and implementation is more likely to achieve the desired aims.

# 2 Design methods

## INTRODUCTION

When we are presented with a problem that requires a computer solution we need a means of converting our ideas into a program. This stage is known as program design. As we shall see later this is not the same thing as writing a program. The first stage in design is analysis. The purpose of this stage is to ensure that we fully understand the problem. Problem statements in English may be ambiguous or unclear. The exact meaning of each of the nouns and and verbs must be defined. Only when we understand what the problem is can we decide on how we are going to solve it.

## DESIGN METHODS

Producing a program which meets the design aims of Chapter 1 cannot be done using an informal trial-and-error approach. We must apply strict engineering standards to our design methods. The chosen method should include a set of rules which must be followed. Various design methods are available to us. Some of the more commonly used methods are:

- Linear
- Evolutionary
- Bottom up
- Top down.

## LINEAR

This method of design involves starting at the beginning of the program and writing the first line, then the second, third, etc., through to the end. It takes no account of the structure of the program. Indeed programs written this way often have little or no structure. Unfortunately some languages, e.g. BASIC, make it easy to produce programs this way. If you are new to programming you may be tempted to produce your first few programs by this method. Resist it! Using this method, our car manufacturer from Chapter 1 would first design the front bumper. Then the headlights, then radiator grill and so on, to finish up with the back bumper.

## EVOLUTIONARY

Using this technique the program just grows and grows almost out of control. You start off with an apparently good program. It does everything asked of it with no bugs. Then perhaps you add an extra section to display in colour. Next you add some more features you had not thought of originally. This process continues, building up the program in a haphazard and unplanned way. Eventually you have a program which may work, but more likely doesn't, though you haven't a clue how it all fits together. Our car manufacturer this time would start off with a go-cart. Then, when it started to rain, he might add a roof. Later perhaps an extra seat is added for a passenger. Now the engine isn't strong enough so a bigger one is squeezed in, and so it goes on.

## BOTTOM UP

With bottom up design we start with the basic, nitty gritty details of the problem and gradually build up to a complete program. Unlike the organic method, the individual sections of the program are brought together in a planned way. The final outcome is known from the start. The car manufacturer using this method may start by designing the bracket that holds the brake pipe in place, after that the brake pipe itself and then the brake shoes, etc.

## TOP DOWN

The top down approach involves taking the whole problem and breaking it down into several smaller problems. Each of these smaller problems is then broken down again into even simpler ones. This process continues until we are left with a whole series of fairly simple problems to solve. When solving these simple problems we can concentrate on a relatively small area of the whole task, this makes the job much simpler and less prone to errors. Top down design of a car would mean breaking the problem down into design of the bodyshell, engine, transmission, suspension, interior, etc. Then further breaking down the engine design into fuel system, ignition system, lubrication, etc. The fuel system can be further divided until we end up with individual parts that can be manufactured.

## WHICH DESIGN METHOD TO USE

The first two methods, namely linear and evolutionary, appear to be the most attractive. Very little forethought or planning is required and a program can be produced quickly. The linear method seems logical, you start at the beginning and work through to the end. The evolutionary method allows you to build up

the program in stages. Adding extra features as you need them. However, as we have seen with our car manufacturer, both of these methods are unsuitable for anything but the smallest of problems. The two other methods, bottom up and top down both follow sound engineering practice. The technique of dividing an object or task into a series of smaller modules and then tackling each module individually is common throughout engineering. This technique is used in both the top down and bottom up design methods, so which do we use? For almost all problems you are likely to encounter the top down method is the most suitable. The bottom up method is a perfectly valid method for a small number of cases where it is essential that the low-level core of the program is designed first. This is sometimes required where the feasibility of the whole program depends on these low level parts. However for most cases top down is the preferred technique, and is the method we will adopt for the rest of this book.

## TOP DOWN DESIGN

The top down method of design is based on the technique of breaking a task down into a series of sub-tasks. Then, taking each sub-task in turn, breaking it down into further sub-tasks. At each stage more detail is added. The top level is a general description of the whole, and the lowest level is a very detailed description of a small part. This is actually a very natural way of working. There are many examples of top down principles in everyday life. Consider a postal address. In top down terms it is written upside down, but could be written.

> The World
> Europe
> Great Britain
> England
> Borsetshire
> Ambridge
> High Street
> 31

Here we start with a very general location (the world) and with each line introduce more detail to eventually pinpoint the location exactly. We could continue by breaking down 31 High Street into rooms and even furniture within a room. Thus, we started with a very general description of a location, i.e. the world, and have successively added more detail at each level until we have a particular chair in a particular room in a particular house, etc. Another example of a top down approach in everyday life is time and date. We break down a year into months, weeks, days, hours, minutes and seconds. So we can describe any particular moment in detail at the lowest level, or more generally at a higher level.

The process of giving increasing detail at each level is known as "stepwise refinement". Stepwise because it is a step-by-step approach. Refinement because at each step we refine, or improve, the level of detail. Stepwise refinement can be used to describe a variety of situations, including a location as we have seen above. When the method is applied to the solution of a problem as a series of tasks and sub-tasks it is sometimes referred to as "functional decomposition".

## FUNCTIONAL DECOMPOSITION

Functional decomposition concentrates on the functions or actions that need to be carried out to solve a problem. The technique is particularly useful in the design of software because a computer program is basically a list of functions or actions that the programmer wishes the computer to carry out.

Using functional decomposition to describe making a cup of tea we could produce a sequence of actions thus:

Make a cup of tea.

Which at the first step refines to.

Prepare the tea pot
Boil the water
Pour water into the pot

Wait for the tea to brew
Pour tea into cup.

At the next step we refine our description of the actions. For example "Boil the water" could be refined to give:

Fill kettle with water
Switch kettle on
Wait until boiled
Switch kettle off.

Similarly "Fill kettle with water" could be further refined to give:

Take kettle to tap
Remove lid
Turn tap on
Wait until full
Turn tap off
Replace lid
Return kettle.

We started with a general problem, "making a cup of tea", and have broken it down into much simpler tasks such as switch kettle off, turn tap on, etc.

Knowing when a problem has been decomposed far enough into simple tasks can be difficult for users new to the technique of functional decomposition. How do we know when we have reached the stage where further refinement is not necessary?

## BUILDING BLOCKS

Functional decomposition is based on the concept of simple building blocks. All problems, to which there is a computer solution, can be solved by an appropriate combination of these simple building blocks. These building blocks are called primitives. They represent the simplest actions that can be performed. Primitives cannot be subdivided further into simpler actions. The number of these primitives is surprisingly few. There are in fact only four, they are:

1. Input data from the outside world.
2. Output data to the outside world.
3. Move data from one storage area to another.
4. Perform a simple one-step calculation.

Taking these in turn we can see their role

1. *Input data from the outside world.* Most computer programs rely on data supplied to them when they are run. This data can come from a number of sources, for example a keyboard, disk file, mouse, light pen, etc. However, at the primitive level we can treat all these the same. The input primitive is only concerned with transferring a single piece of data from outside the program to a storage area within the program. This is its only function, no modification or processing of the data takes place.

2. *Output data to the outside world.* All useful programs produce an output of some kind. If no output has been produced then the program has had no effect. As with input, output may be to one of a number of devices. The output primitive only involves the transfer of a single piece of data from within the program to the outside world. The outside world in this context means anywhere not within the program. Again, no modification or processing of the data takes place.

3. *Move data from one storage area to another.* Sometimes within a program it is necessary to have more than one copy of a piece of data. Taking a second copy is achieved by moving the data to another storage area. This moving action does not alter or delete the original data, it simply creates a second identical copy.

4. *Perform a simple one-step calculation.* This is probably the area which causes the novice most problems. What is a single-step calculation? Strictly, it is performing either addition, subtraction, multiplication or division on a single pair of numbers. Therefore the following are single-step calculations:

$$8 + 7$$
$$14.6 - 11.56$$
$$24.1 * 6$$
$$100 / 5$$

However, most practical programming systems allow for simple combinations of these

to be considered as a single step. For example

$$8 + 7 - 5$$
$$2 * 4 + 3$$

It must be realized though that these actions are not strictly primitives since they can be further divided. Also most programming systems allow common mathematical functions such as square root, cosine, logarithm, etc., to be treated as primitives. These clearly are more than simple one-step actions. Because of their usefulness and the frequency with which they are needed they are usually provided as one-step library functions. Library functions are described in more detail in the next chapter.

# DESIGN METHODOLOGIES

Having decided to use top down as a design technique we need some method of recording our choices of tasks and sub-tasks. We also need to show how the various sub-tasks are connected together.

Several different methods are available. Three, of the most popular are structure diagrams, modular flowcharts and pseudocode. We will investigate each of these three in turn and see how they can help in top down design.

# STRUCTURE DIAGRAMS

Structure diagrams were first introduced by Michael Jackson as part of his technique known as Jackson's Structured Design (JSD). It is a top down technique where the whole task is first represented by a single box. This is then broken down into sub-tasks which are shown as boxes below the first box. The sub-tasks may then be further broken down which is represented by another layer below. All the modules connected below a module are known as its child modules. The module connected above any module is its parent module. In Fig. 2.1, B, C and D are child modules of A. A is the parent module for B, C and D. Modules E and F are child modules of C.

The modules, represented by boxes, at each level can be one of three different types.

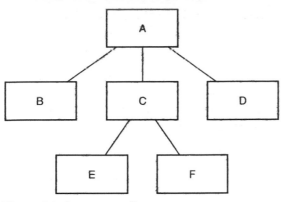

Figure 2.1 A structure diagram.

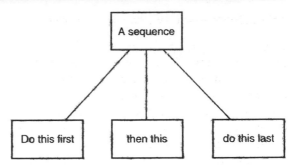

Figure 2.2 A sequence.

The allowed types are sequence, selection and iteration. These three concepts are present in all top down design techniques, and we shall meet them again when we consider programming languages.

## Sequence

A sequence is a series of steps, or actions, which is carried out in order. That is, there is a time-related relationship between the actions. On structure diagrams, time flows from left to right. So a sequence of three actions can be shown as in Fig. 2.2.

We have broken down "a sequence" into three parts. Each part is represented by a box. The actions in the boxes are carried out in order from left to right. It is important to note that the box, "a sequence", consists of all three of the actions, i.e. the lower three boxes can be thought of as being "inside" the upper box.

Each of the lower boxes could be broken down further to show more detail if necessary. If a box does need to be broken down further this can be done on the same diagram, to give another level, or drawn on another diagram with the module as the topmost box. As a general rule there should be no more than three or four levels on a diagram. More levels than this and the diagram tends to become cluttered and difficult to understand. Therefore, except for simple problems, most structure diagrams occupy several sheets of paper. This has an advantage for someone other than the originator reading the diagram. If only a general idea of the structure is required the top level diagram is sufficient, but if detailed information of a particular module is required then the lower levels can be consulted.

To show how a problem can be broken down layer by layer we will return to the cup of tea example. Figure 2.3 shows a possible top level diagram.

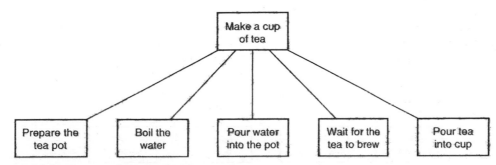

Figure 2.3 Making a cup of tea: top level.

This shows each of the five actions in a logical sequence. In order to solve the problem (i.e. make a cup of tea) the actions must be carried out in this order. At this level of detail we have shown **what** must be done. We have not shown **how** to carry out each of the actions. To give more detail some, or all, of the boxes could be decomposed further. The box labelled "boil the water" could be decomposed as in Fig. 2.4.

This could be as another level on the same diagram, or as a separate diagram. When deciding whether or not to create a separate diagram several factors need to be considered. Is there enough room on the paper? Remember the other boxes at this level may also need decomposing. Does the box represent a whole entity, or function, that is worth considering separately. Is this a convenient and logical place to break the design?

Taking each box in turn and decomposing it to show more detail continues until, at the lowest level, the boxes represent the primitive actions discussed earlier.

Making a cup of tea illustrates the technique of structure diagrams but it is not the sort of problem we are likely to be writing a program to solve. Suppose we wish to find the average value of three numbers. Mathematically this is given by dividing the sum of the numbers by the number of numbers, in this case three. This function is clearly not a primitive so we will need to decompose it into its primitives. As a starting point we can identify three actions which must be carried out in a sequence.

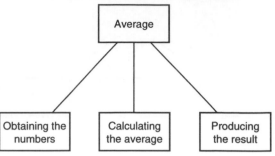

**Figure 2.5** The average problem: top level.

> Obtain the numbers
> Calculate the average
> Produce the result.

This initial breakdown into "get the inputs", "do the calculation", "produce the output", is a good starting point for many simple problems. Figure 2.5 shows this.

The action "obtain the numbers" could be further broken down as shown in Fig. 2.6.

Calculating the average consists of two actions. These are to sum the numbers together and to divide the sum by three. Figure 2.7 completes the solution.

## Selection

So far we have only been able to represent a straightforward sequence of actions. All the actions must be performed in the same order. We may need to represent two, or more, alternative actions. We also could have a situation where we wish to either perform an action or not perform it. For these cases we use selection.

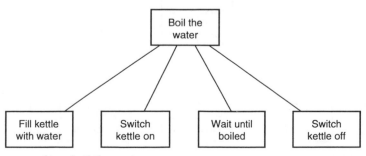

**Figure 2.4** Making a cup of tea: boil the water.

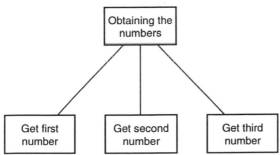

Figure 2.6 The average problem: obtaining the numbers.

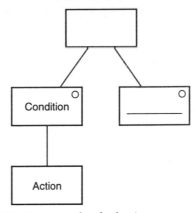

Figure 2.8 An example of selection.

Selection allows for one of a number of possible actions to be chosen to be performed under specified circumstances. This is represented on a structure diagram by a small circle in the top right-hand corner of the box.

There are three possible types of selection:

1. Choosing to perform an action or not to perform it.
2. Choosing to perform an action or otherwise perform a different action.
3. Choosing to perform one of a set of possible alternative actions.

In each case the selection depends upon a condition being either true or false.

In the first case the logic is

"If the condition is true then perform the action, otherwise do nothing".

This is shown using a structure chart in Fig. 2.8.

In the second case:

"If the condition is true then perform this action, otherwise perform that action."

On the structure diagram this is shown by entering the alternative action in the right-most box as shown in Fig. 2.9. Note that either, or both, of the boxes could be further decomposed to give more detail of the required actions.

The third case is a multi-way selection, where one, and only one, of a number of choices is to be made based upon various conditions. This could be described as; "If condition 1 is true then do action 1, otherwise if condition 2 is true then do action 2, otherwise if condition 3 is true then do action 3, otherwise if condition 4 is true then do action 4, otherwise", . . . , etc.

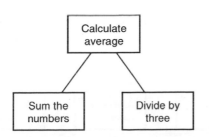

Figure 2.7 The average problem: calculate average

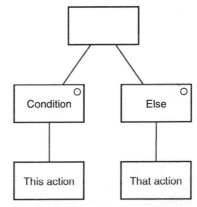

Figure 2.9 Selection with alternative action.

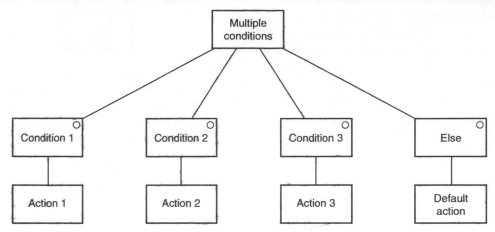

**Figure 2.10** Multiway selection.

Figure 2.10 shows how this is represented on the structure diagram. There may or may not be an "else" box. If there is, the convention is to make the right-most box the "else". If there is no "else" box and none of the conditions are true then no action is performed.

Multiple selections can be shown by decomposing one box of a selection to further selections. For example the statement "Salaries are paid on the third Thursday of the month" is illustrated in Fig. 2.11.

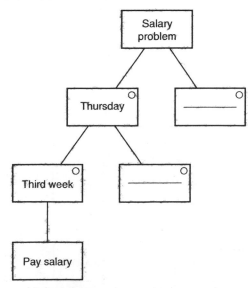

**Figure 2.11** Multiple selection.

## Iteration

Often the computer solution to a problem is based on performing the same task many times. Computers are particularly good at working this way, whereas humans are particularly bad. We quickly become bored at a repetitive task. On a structure diagram we use a special symbol to show that an action may to be performed a number of times. A small star is placed in the top right-hand corner of the box.

Within the box details of the condition controlling the number of iterations are given. This usually takes one of three forms:

1. A fixed number of repetitions, e.g. 100.
2. Repeat while some condition is true, e.g. WHILE value < 6
3. Repeat until some condition becomes true, e.g. UNTIL end of list.

In each case the same symbol is used and a written description is placed in the box. Figure 2.12 shows some examples of iteration.

We can now combine sequence, selection and iteration in the solution of a real problem.

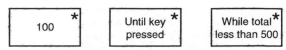

**Figure 2.12** Examples of iteration.

Imagine the situation where we have the results of twenty students who have sat an exam. The pass mark for the exam is fifty percent. We wish to know how many students have passed and how many have failed. We start with one box representing the whole problem.

This can be broken down into a sequence of two actions, "process the marks", and "produce the results". The first of these can itself be thought of as a sequence of two actions, "initial processing" and "further processing".

The initial processing sets up two counters, one for the passes and one for the fails. The further processing actually reads and processes the exam marks. Clearly this has to be an iteration of twenty times. Figure 2.13 illustrates the exam mark problem.

## Dos and don'ts

There are several rules governing the layout of structure diagrams. These are designed to aid clarity and understanding, and to remove any ambiguity. The first rule concerns the connections between modules. It states that all modules, except the top level module, must have one and only one parent module. We think of a module actually being a more detailed description of part of its parent. It is therefore effectively inside its parent. Clearly it cannot be inside two parent modules. If a module is required to be a child of two different parents then it must appear twice on the diagram.

The second rule concerns the child modules of any parent. All the child modules must be of the same type, i.e. sequence, selection or iteration. Mixing the three types on any level is not permitted. This rule sometimes requires the introduction of dummy modules. Consider a case involving three actions X, Y and Z. Action X is to be performed once, followed by Y and the action Z repeated four times. One description of this may be given by Fig. 2.14. However this breaks the rule. To produce a correct diagram the extra, dummy module Q is introduced in Fig. 2.15. Now all the child modules of the top level are of the same type, sequence.

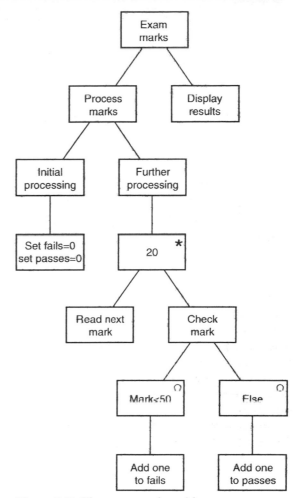

Figure 2.13 The exam mark problem.

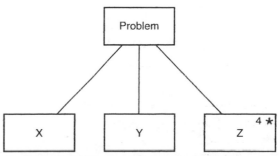

Figure 2.14 An incorrect structure diagram.

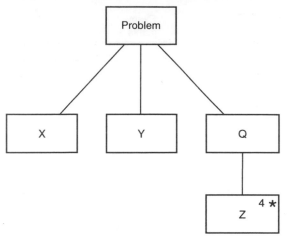

**Figure 2.15** The corrected structure diagram.

Figure 2.16 breaks both of the rules and is unacceptable as a structure diagram.

## MODULAR FLOWCHARTS

Structure diagrams show the overall structure of a solution. The individual modules are clearly identified and the relationships between them formalized. Sometimes, however, it is easier to understand a solution as a flow of events or actions. The alternative graphical design technique known as modular, or structured, flowcharts can be used. Modular flowcharting is a top down method. The technique is a development from traditional flowcharts.

Traditional flowcharts use a set of symbols to represent events and actions. These symbols are connected by lines. The lines show the flow of the program from one action to the next. At any point in the flowchart the only allowable actions are those which are connected to the current point by a line. Traditional flowchart methods impose no restrictions on how the symbols may be connected together. These can lead to large and complicated diagrams with many interconnecting and crossing lines. Programs produced this way tend to be cumbersome and unstructured, often called "spaghetti code".

Modular flowcharting restricts the ways in

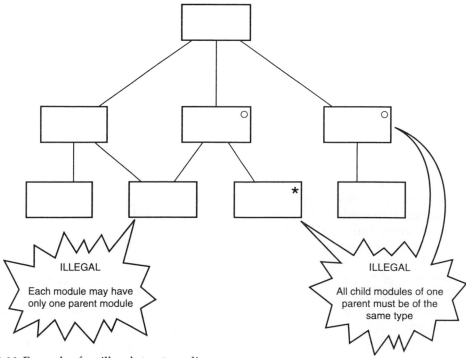

**Figure 2.16** Example of an illegal structure diagram.

which the symbols may be connected together. This results in a small number of standard "shapes" which are used as building blocks. These standard modules have a characteristic in common which enables us to use a structured top down approach. Each module has only one entry point and only one exit point.

Figure 2.17 shows the symbols used in modular flowcharts

All modules start and end with a terminator symbol. It is conventional to put the name of the module in the start terminator. There is no need to to put "exit" or "end" in the finish terminator. An empty terminator is always a module exit.

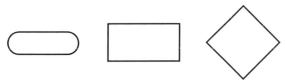

**Figure 2.17** Modular flowchart symbols.

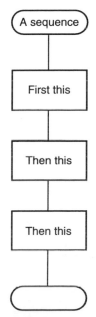

**Figure 2.18** A sequence.

## Sequence

A sequence of actions is shown as two or more modules, one beneath another, joined by lines. Therefore the flow of time is down the chart. Figure 2.18 illustrates a sequence.

## Selection

As with structure diagrams there are three forms of the selection chart. With selection the diamond-shaped symbol is used to show the condition upon which the selection is made. The diamond has two exits. These are usually labelled "Y" and "N" to represent "yes" and "no". The condition in the diamond must be one which gives only a yes or no answer.

### Simple two-way selections

There are two forms. The first is selecting to perform an action or miss it out. That is "If the condition is true then perform the action, otherwise do nothing".

The second is selecting to perform one action, or alternatively to perform a different action. This is expressed as:

> "If the condition is true then perform this action, otherwise perform that action."

These are shown in Figs 2.19 and 2.20.

### Multi-way selections

The multi-way selection is shown in Fig. 2.21. The condition which governs each selection is given above the corresponding branch from the main horizontal line.

Note it is very important that in modular flowcharts the flow lines after the selected actions must rejoin into one line before the finish terminator. With traditional flowcharts the flow lines leaving a diamond may be connected to anywhere, this is not so with modular flowcharts.

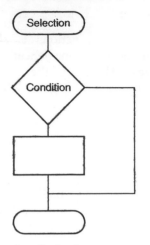

Figure 2.19 Examples of selection.

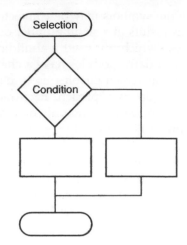

Figure 2.20

## Iteration

There are two forms of modular flowchart which can be used to show iteration. These are given in Fig. 2.22. The important difference is whether the test comes before or after the action. The test is to check whether another iteration is required. In Fig. 2.22(a) the test is performed after the action. In this case the action will always be performed at least once. In Fig. 2.22(b) the test is performed before the action. If the test fails the first time then we have an iteration of zero. Some solutions to problems require that zero iterations is a valid case. For these solutions flowcharts of the form of Fig. 2.22(b) must be used. Most often Fig. 2.22(a) is the appropriate form.

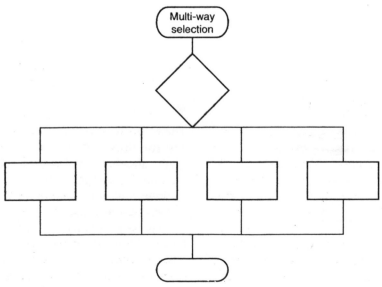

Figure 2.21 Multiway selection.

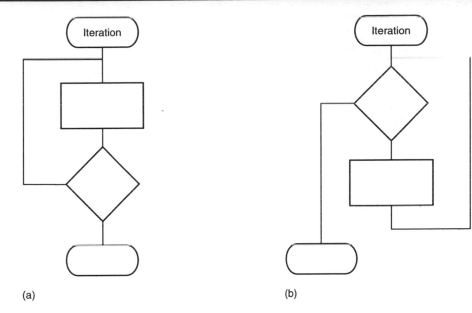

(a)                                    (b)

**Figure 2.22.**

## Connecting modules together

Modular flowcharting is a top down method therefore we need way of showing the hierarchy of modules. This is done by expanding the rectangular, action boxes to give more detail on another flowchart. An action box can be expanded into any of the standard shapes of sequence, selection and iteration. We can think of any of the standard shapes actually fitting inside the module box. Each module is decomposed to give more detail on another flowchart. Figure 2.23 shows this diagrammatically.

The link between a module and its expansion is provided by the name. The name of the module is written in the box and the same name is written in the entry terminator of the expansion. In large and complex systems the flowcharts can cover many pages. To aid in identifying the correct links the page number of the expansion is sometimes also put in the module box. Expansion continues, perhaps through several levels, until the module boxes represent the primitive actions discussed earlier.

Taking the exam results problem from page 13, we have: produced a modular flowchart design (see Fig. 2.24).

## Dos and don'ts

There are several rules governing how modular flowcharts should be drawn. These are designed to improve clarity and avoid ambiguity.

The main flow should always be from top to bottom. In particular the entry point for a module is always at the top and the exit is always at the bottom. As with all forms of modular, top down, design each module must have only one entry point and one exit point. This ensures that any module may be nested inside any other module.

In general, each module should consist of one of the shapes described above. However, it is permissible to combine two modules onto one diagram if it improves the clarity. The two must be combined in such a way that they could be drawn separately. Figure 2.25 shows two selection modules combined correctly on one diagram. The flowchart shown in Fig. 2.26

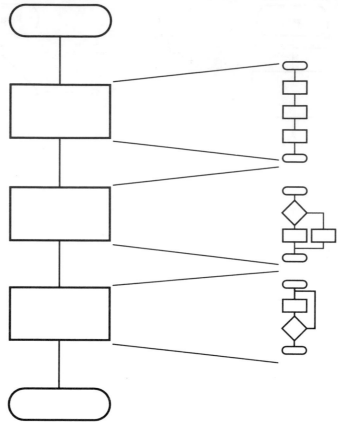

**Figure 2.23** "Nesting" of modules.

is not properly structured as it cannot be broken down into two correctly formed modules. Care must be taken when showing a loop nested inside another loop on a single diagram. Figures 2.27 and 2.28 show this correctly and incorrectly respectively. There is no rule concerning which exit is "yes" and which is "no" on a selection diamond, but it is usually clearer if the most likely result is straight down and the less likely to the side. Clearly sometimes the two are of equal likelihood, in this case the choice is immaterial.

## PSEUDOCODE

Pseudocode, also known as Program Design Language (PDL) or structured English, is used to express program design verbally rather than diagrammatically. It uses a sequence of sentences and allows for:

- Statements to be written in free English text, they may be as complex as required but conciseness and brevity is desirable.
- The use of only three structures, namely sequence, selection and repetition.
- An easy translation from design to implementation in a programming language.

Pseudocode was originally developed by assembly language programmers as a means of expressing the structure and logic of programs in a natural and easily understood manner. The advantages are:

- It allows us to express design details using the freedom of a native language.
- It allows us to develop and express a design without worrying about language details such as syntax.
- It can be easily generated and maintained using any text editor or word processor.

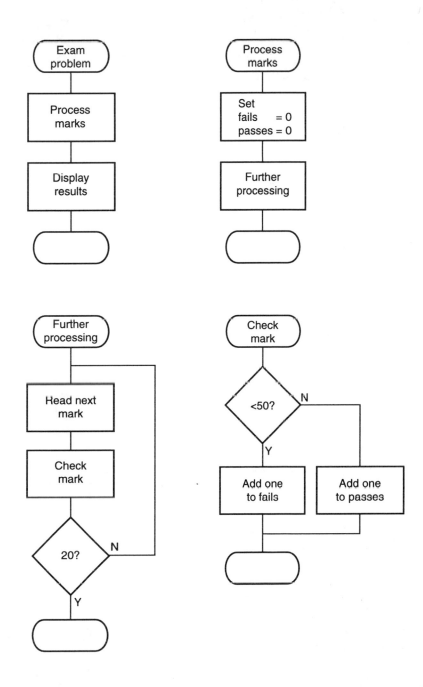

**Figure 2.24**

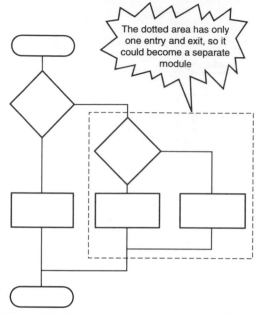

**Figure 2.25** Two modules combined legally.

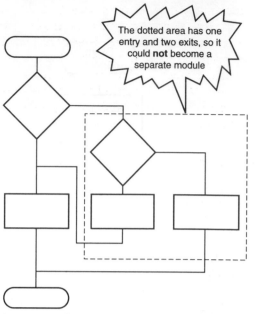

**Figure 2.26** Illegal combination of selection modules.

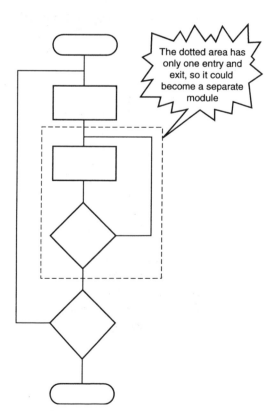

**Figure 2.27** Correctly nested iteration modules.

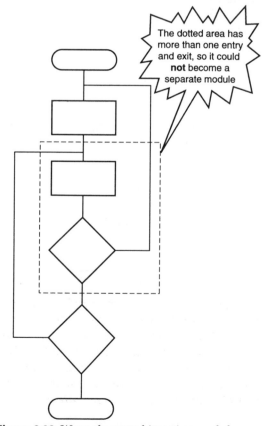

**Figure 2.28** Wrongly nested iteration modules.

Pseudocode which is truly free format can lead to the same problems as traditional, unstructured flowcharts. Therefore when using pseudocode in a top down, structured approach certain limitations are imposed. These are designed to incorporate the same basic structures as in modular flowcharts and structure diagrams.

## General structure

In top down pseudocode design each step is expanded until it is at a sufficient level to be implemented as a programming language primitive.

## Sequence

A sequence of actions is denoted by simply writing the actions one underneath the other. If a task requires three actions to be performed in the order Action1, Action2 and Action3 then a pseudocode representation of the task would be:

> Action1
> Action2
> Action3

If Action2 needs to be broken down further into three sub-actions, a, b and c, then this is shown as:

> Action1
> Action2
>   Action2a
>   Action2b
>   Action2c
> Action3

Note the indentation from the left. Indentation is used to show the grouping together of actions at each level. Some users of pseudocode also advocate numbering to aid clarity. Each action is given a number and subdivisions are numbered with a decimal point separating the number from its parent

1. Action1
2. Action2
  2.1. Action2a
  2.2. Action2b
  2.3. Action2c
3. Action3

If Action2c needs to be divided into two more actions this is represented as:

1. Action1
2. Action2
  2.1. Action2a
  2.2. Action2b
  2.3. Action2c
    2.3.1. Action2c1
    2.3.2. Action2c2
3. Action3

The use of numbers can be a disadvantage because it disrupts the natural flow of the language used. The decision whether or not to use numbers is a personal one.

Expressing the making a cup of tea problem in pseudocode gives us:

> Make a cup of tea.
>   Prepare the tea pot
>   Boil the water
>     Fill kettle with water
>       Take kettle to tap
>       Remove lid
>       Turn tap on
>       Wait until full
>       Turn tap off
>       Replace lid
>       Return kettle
>     Switch kettle on
>     Wait until boiled
>     Switch kettle off
>   Pour water into the pot
>   Wait for the tea to brew
>   Pour tea into cup.

## Selection

The selection construct takes several forms. The simplest is when an action needs to be either performed or not performed. This has the general form

> if <condition> then <action> endif

where <condition> is any expression which evaluates to only TRUE or FALSE, and <action> is the action to be performed if the expression is true.

For example supposing we wish to add a number to a total if the number is greater than ten. This can be expressed in pseudocode as:

> if number > 10 then
> add number to total
> endif

The action to be performed may be a sequence of simpler actions. In this case the indentation is used to show the structure. For example

> if number > 10 then
> add number to total
> square number
> print square
> endif

The second form of selection is where a choice between two alternative actions is to be made. This has the general form:

> if <condition> then
> <first action>
> else
> <second action>
> endif

If the condition is true the the first action is performed, but if it is false then the second action is performed instead. One, and only one, of the actions is always carried out. For example

> if number < 100 then
> print "Too small"
> else
> print "Too big"
> endif

As before the first action and the second action may be expanded to a sequence of actions.

Multiple selection, that is one choice from several options, can be represented in one of two ways. It can be represented as several if ... then ... else ... endif statements. For example

> if age < 18 then
> print "Too young"
> else
> if age > 65 then
> print "Too old"
> else
> print "O.K."
> endif
> endif

Because this type of construct is very common and useful in programming some pseudocode practitioners use an extra word "elsif" to combine the else and if. The example above could be expressed thus:

> if age < 18 then
> print "Too young"
> elsif age > 65 then
> print "Too old"
> else
> print "O.K."
> endif

This has the advantage of simplifying the indentation and reducing the number of endifs, useful if the number of choices exceeds four or five. Either method may be used, but it is less confusing if only one method is used within a particular design.

## Iteration

As with the two other design methods we have met, pseudocode has several ways of expressing iteration or repetition. The simplest of these is where an action, or sequence of actions, needs to be repeated a fixed number of times. The general form is

> loop for n times
> Action(s) to be carried out
> repeat

In this case the actions(s) will be performed *n* times. If we wished to calculate the total of fifteen numbers this could be expressed as

    set total to 0
    loop for 15 times
        get next number
        add number to total
    repeat

The other forms of iteration loop can be generalized as

    loop while a condition exists
        Actions(s) to be carried out
    repeat

and

    repeat
        Actions(s) to be carried out
    loop while a condition exists

In the first case the test to see if another iteration is required is done before the action(s). In the second case the test is done after the action(s).

The condition controlling the iteration loop depends on the nature of the problem. Typically the condition tests to see if some variable is less than, equal to or greater than a constant. Any statement which can be evaluated to only true or false may be used.

We can now combine sequence, selection and iteration into a pseudocode solution for the exam results problem on page 13.

    Process marks
        Initial processing
            set number of fails to zero
            set number of passes to zero
        Further processing
            loop for 20 times
                read next mark
                if mark < 50 then
                    add one to number of fails
                else
                    add one to number of passes
            repeat

    Display results
        print number of passes
        print number of fails

## A DESIGN EXERCISE

Having studied the three design methods we are now in a position to produce a program design from a specification. We can do this for each of the three methods. The basic structure of the solution will be the same for each design method. The only difference is the way it is represented.

### Problem

Design a program to read the weight of an item as a value in pounds and ounces and display the weight in kilogrammes. The values for pounds and ounces will always be whole numbers.

### Solution

The problem can be broken down into a sequence of three actions.

    Read the input data
    Calculate the answer
    Display the results

### Structure chart solution

Figure 2.29 shows a structure chart solution to the problem.

Figure 2.30 shows a modular flowchart solution to the problem.

### Pseudocode solution

    Get the input data
        Input the pounds value
        Input the ounces value
    Calculate the answer
        Multiply the pounds by 16
        Add the pounds and ounces
        Kilos value = ounces/35.2
    Display the results
        Display kilos value

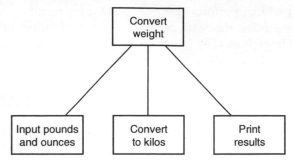

**Figure 2.29** Structure chart solution.

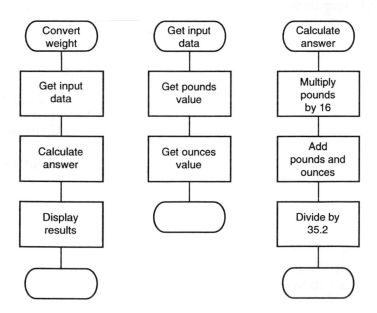

**Figure 2.30**

## SUMMARY

❑ Using a good structured design method is crucial to the success of a software project.

❑ Top down modular design is the preferred technique.

❑ All designs can be constructed solely of three elements: sequence, selection and iteration.

❑ The design may be realized using structure charts, modular flowcharts or pseudocode.

## EXERCISES

1. Produce a structured design for a solution to the following:

   A program is required to read ten numbers and produce an output showing the number of positive numbers, the number of negative numbers, the largest number and the smallest number.

2. Using modular flowcharts, a structure diagram or pseudocode design a program to solve the following problem:

   A survey has been carried out of the number of cars crossing the Severn Bridge. The number of cars crossing during each hour is recorded, giving 24 counts per day.

   The program is to read the counts for one day and produce an output giving the total number of cars crossing during the day and the maximum crossing in any hour.

# 3 Programming languages

## INTRODUCTION

In order to perform any useful task a computer system must have two components: hardware and software. The hardware is all the electronic and mechanical equipment, i.e. those parts that can be seen and touched. The software can neither be seen nor touched but is an equally essential part. Software is a general term used to describe the stored instructions which the computer uses to perform a specific task. Computers are general-purpose machines. Often the manufacturers have no idea of the use to which their products will be put. The user of the computer determines what it will be used for. It is the software which provides this flexibility. Computers with identical hardware can be made to perform very different tasks by having different software. It is programming that produces the software.

## COMPUTER LANGUAGES

Languages are a form of communication. When we wish to communicate with another person we may use one of a number of different languages. For written or spoken communication we use a natural language such as English, Spanish or Urdu. To communicate visually we could use a visual language such sign language or semaphore. If both sender and receiver understand the language then communication can be achieved. We can use a simple language to communicate with an animal such as a dog. By using words like "sit", "heel" and "stay" we can communicate with the dog. The dog has only a limited number of commands which it can understand. But by giving it a sequence of simple commands the dog can be made to perform more complex tasks.

We also use languages to communicate with computers. There are many different computer languages, each designed to communicate with a computer at a particular level, or to communicate a particular type of information. The simplest, lowest level languages are designed to communicate directly with the computer's electronics. The most complex, highest level, languages are similar to natural languages. Commands in high level languages need to be translated into the lower level language before the computer can act upon them.

## LOW LEVEL LANGUAGES

In its simplest form a computer program consists of a list of instructions for the computer to carry out. The instructions are stored within the computers memory. They are read, one at a time, from the memory and acted upon by the central processing unit (CPU). The CPU can only recognize a limited number of instructions. These are termed the instruction set of the CPU. Each instruction is allocated a unique numerical code. It is these numbers,

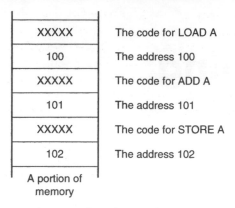

| | |
|---|---|
| XXXXX | The code for LOAD A |
| 100 | The address 100 |
| XXXXX | The code for ADD A |
| 101 | The address 101 |
| XXXXX | The code for STORE A |
| 102 | The address 102 |

A portion of memory

**Figure 3.1** Storage of machine code instructions.

stored in binary form, which make up the program.

When a program is 'run' the first instruction is fetched from the memory to the CPU. The CPU then executes, or carries out, the instruction. When execution is complete the next instruction in the program is fetched. This instruction is then executed. The process continues, fetching and executing each instruction in turn. This is known as the fetch–execute cycle. All digital computers work on this simple principle. Programs are made up of many of these simple instructions. There may be thousands, or even millions, of instructions in a program. Modern CPUs execute instructions very fast, perhaps more than a million per second. In this way a complex task made up of many

simple instructions can be performed in a very short time by human standards.

## Machine code

Instructions are stored electronically in the computers memory as binary codes. Each instruction is stored in a separate location which is given a unique address. Figure 3.1 shows how a program segment is stored. Each binary code, representing an instruction, is decoded by the CPU electronics and the signals produced to carry out the required action.

The computer can only "understand" programs made up of these binary codes. Each different manufacturers' CPU has a different instruction set and different codes. Therefore programs written this way are machine specific. If they are transferred to a different machine, with a different CPU, they will not execute correctly without modification. Machine code programs are not portable.

Machine code programs written in binary are very difficult to read and understand. It is very easy to make mistakes when reading or writing a long series of ones and noughts. To make it easier to read and less prone to errors programmers use various codes to represent the binary ones and noughts. Hexadecimal code and octal code are the most popular. Figure 3.2 shows examples of these codes. Using hexadecimal notation improves the readability and reduces errors. However, the

| | Decimal | Octal | Hexadecimal | Binary |
|---|---|---|---|---|
| Fifty seven | 57 | 71 | 39 | 111001 |
| Nine | 9 | 11 | 9 | 1001 |
| One hundred and seven | 107 | 153 | 6B | 1101011 |
| Fourteen | 14 | 16 | E | 1110 |
| Twenty three | 23 | 27 | 17 | 11110 |

**Figure 3.2** Comparison of number codes.

programmer still needs to either remember, or look up, the numeric codes for each instruction. Remember that a program may contain many thousands of instructions, so writing or reading a program in machine code is a very difficult task indeed.

## Assembly language

In the early days of electronic computers it became clear that no progress could be made by programming in machine code. The first development in program languages was to use mnemonics (or memory aids) to represent each instruction. These mnemonics were single words or abbreviations chosen to represent the action of each instruction. The machine code program in Fig. 3.1 could be represented thus:

```
LOAD A, 100
ADD A, 101
STORE A, 102
```

Clearly this form of the program is much easier to read and understand. The computer however can only execute the machine code version. So the programmer has to translate the mnemonics into their machine code equivalents before the program can be run. This was usually done by looking up the codes in a table. This process was known as assembling the program. Programs written

this way are said to be written in assembly language or assembler. It was soon realized that the translation from assembly language to machine code was a simple look up process that could be done by a computer program. The programmer can then concentrate on writing the assembly language program and use the computer itself to perform the translation to machine code. The program which performs this translation is called an assembler. The translation process is illustrated in Fig. 3.3.

Modern assemblers provide more than just mnemonic to machine code translation. Addresses used by the programmer to identify sections of program or data storage locations can be given names. These names are known as symbolic addresses. The assembler allocates a memory address for each symbolic address in the program. The programmer can use meaningful names, such as "length", "average" or "voltage", rather than numeric addresses. Programs using symbolic addresses are more readable and less prone to errors. The program from Fig. 3.1 could be written

```
Calculate:  LOAD A, Costprice
            ADD A, Markup
            STORE A, Saleprice
```

The use of mnemonics and symbolic addresses make assembly language programs much easier to develop and maintain than machine code. If an assembler is available there is no need to use machine code at all. However, the programmer still needs a detailed knowledge of the CPU's instruction set and the number and arrangement of the internal registers. To produce complex programs in assembly language is a considerable task requiring a skilled and experienced programmer.

Assembly language is closely related to machine code. For each assembly language instruction there is a corresponding machine code instruction. This is known as a one-to-one translation. Machine code and assembly language are both examples of a "low level" language. This term is applied as the language is essentially at the same level as the hardware of the computer.

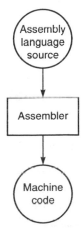

**Figure 3.3** Role of the assembler.

# HIGH LEVEL LANGUAGES

Low level languages are essentially machine orientated. A low level language describes **how** the computer can be used to solve a problem. It is concerned with the detailed actions the computer needs to perform. This approach limits program writing to those with a detailed understanding of computers. This problem was recognized early on in the development of computing and led to the development of high level languages. A high level language is problem orientated. The language is used to describe a solution to a problem, and is not concerned with how the computer carries it out. A high level language program describes **what** has to be done, but not **how** it is to be done.

All the early high level languages were designed to be used to solve mathematical and scientific problems. They were based around the evaluation of formulae or arithmetic expressions. The concept of symbolic addressing was extended to cover mathematical variables, which traditionally in algebra are given letters or symbols. So high level languages be used to calculate expressions such as:

$$A + B \times C$$

The normal rules of algebra are used including the use of brackets. In most languages the symbolic names may be whole words which improves the readability. For example

saleprice = costprice + markup
perimeter = 2 × (length + width).

Additional commands are used to control the order in which the actions are performed. These commands are actual English words such as "if", "while", "end", etc. A program written in a high level language reflects more closely the way a person sees the program, than the way the computer solves it. The programmer does not need to know how the computer operates. This opens up programming to those without an understanding of how computers work. It is arguable that if it were not for the development of high level languages, computers would not have gained the widespread use that they have today.

# LANGUAGE TRANSLATION

As explained earlier the computer only recognizes programs in machine code. Programs written in any other language have to be translated into machine code before they can be run. This translation is usually done automatically using a program specially written for the purpose.

## Assembly language

Assembly language programs are translated by the assembler. The assembler's job is two-fold:

1. To translate each instruction mnemonic to its equivalent machine code.
2. To resolve references to symbolic addresses into actual addresses.

This is usually done by a "two pass" process. The assembler reads the program source text twice. The first time the assembler makes a list of all the symbolic names used in the program and their actual addresses. The second time the source text is read the instructions are translated, if reference is made to a symbolic name its actual value is read from the list and substituted in the machine code. Figure 3.4 shows this process.

## High level language translators

The function of a translator is two-fold. First it needs to check that the program is written correctly. It must make sure that the program does not break any of the rules of the language. The rules of a language are known as its syntax.

# LANGUAGE SYNTAX

All languages, natural and computer, have rules. The rules of English govern the way nouns, adjectives, prepositions, etc., are put together to form grammatically correct sentences. The rules, or syntax, of a computer language govern the way the various elements of the language are put together to form programs. With natural languages the

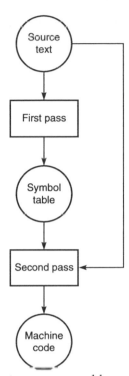

**Figure 3.4** The two pass assembly process.

rules are fairly flexible, often a matter of 'good grammar' and 'bad grammar' rather than right and wrong. Also a human reader can read an incorrectly structured English sentence and still deduce its meaning. High level language translators, however, require strict adherence to the syntax rules of the language. If a program does not follow these rules then it is said to have syntax errors. A program which has syntax errors cannot be "understood" by the translator, and so it cannot determine the machine code instructions which the high level program represents.

## Compilers and interpreters

The mechanism for translating high level languages is much more complex than low level assembly and, to a certain extent, varies from language to language. There are two main types of translator used with high level languages:

1. A compiler,
2. An interpreter.

They both appear to perform a similar function, but the difference can be very important.

Translation of one computer language, or level of language, to another is much like translation of one natural, spoken language to another. The same program written in two computer languages may look very different, though the programs perform the same function. A sentence written in English may look very different when translated into Spanish or Russian, but it has the same meaning.

Imagine you have a task to perform. The instructions for the task are written on a piece of paper, in Spanish. You also have available the services of a Spanish-to-English translator. There are two methods you could use to complete the task.

The first involves giving the list of instructions (in Spanish) to the translator and asking them to rewrite the instructions in English. You are then given back another piece of paper with the translated (English) instructions on it. You can now perform the task without further need for the translator.

For the second method you ask the translator to take the first instruction, translate it and read it out to you in English. You then carry out that instruction. The translator then translates and reads out the next instruction and you carry it out. You continue in this fashion until the task is complete.

The first of these methods, where the whole list is translated and a second copy made, is similar to the way a compiler works. The second method where, each instruction is translated and then performed immediately without writing down the translated copy, is similar to an interpreter's mode of operation. Each method has advantages and disadvantages.

If an interpreter is used then making changes to the program is quicker and easier. It usually entails simply editing the source and then typing a command such as "RUN". Making changes to a compiled program involve editing the source text, running the compiler, and possibly a separate linker, then running the program.

The run time performance of compiled and interpreted programs vary greatly. Because the interpreter has to translate each line as the program is run, interpreted programs generally run slower than compiled programs. This is particularly so for programs with many loops in them. If a particular line in a program is executed twenty times in a loop, the the interpreter will check for correctness and also translate the high level code twenty times.

Finding syntax errors (see above) in a compiled program is much more reliable. A compiler checks the whole program for errors at the compile stage. Most compilers will not generate any machine code for a program containing errors. Therefore if a program can be run then it contains no syntax errors (but see logical errors in Chapter 9). An interpreter only checks the correctness of each line of the program as it runs it. Therefore syntax errors are not found until the program is run. It is possible for an error to remain undetected in an interpreted program, perhaps only being discovered after the program has been in use for many months.

A program which has been compiled into machine code is a stand alone product. Neither the compiler nor the original source text is required to be present when the program is run. When an interpreted program is run however, the interpreter must be present as well. Also, as there is no machine code version, the program must be present in source code form. This has two implications. For a program to be interpreted the host computer must have enough memory to hold both the program and the interpreter at the same time. This limits the size of interpreted programs. Secondly a software author cannot distribute an interpreted program in a stand alone form. The user must also have the appropriate interpreter. Most software authors prefer not to publish their source code, with compiled programs this is not necessary, but an interpreted program is usually run from the source. Some interpreter systems allow an encrypted version of the code to be used, thus protecting the confidentiality of the authors work.

# LANGUAGE LIBRARIES

Most language systems that employ a compiler rather than an interpreter also use something called a linker. The high level language source code is converted by the compiler into object code. However the object code is not the complete program. The object code contains references to sections of code, and also possibly items of data, that are stored in libraries. A library in this sense is a collection of related program segments which may be "borrowed" by other programs. The most common use for library modules is for system specific functions such as accessing input/output peripherals or reading and writing files, etc. These functions are required by most programs. If they are not provided in a library then they have to be included in every program. Library functions can also be used to hide some of the system specific detail from the programmer. For example, a programmer may use a library routine called "readchar" to read a character from the keyboard. The details of the hardware keyboard interface are hidden from the programmer. On a system with different hardware a routine of the same name could be provided which performs the same function. In this way library routines can be used to increase the portability of a program.

After the compiling stage the linker takes the object program and converts it to machine code form. If any reference is made to library functions then the appropriate library is searched and a copy of the required routines is added to the program. The links between the program and the library functions are inserted in the machine code by the linker. Use of a linker enables a program to be written as several modules. Each module can be compiled separately then linked together to form a complete program. In this way several programmers can work in parallel, each on a separate module, so decreasing the development time. Figure 3.5 shows the process of producing an executable program from a high level language source text.

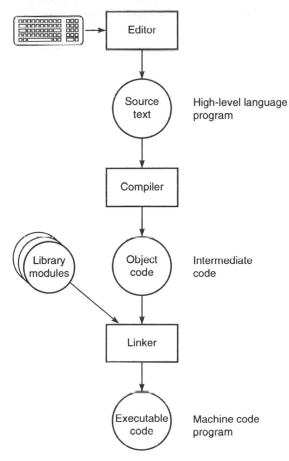

**Figure 3.5** Producing an executable program using a high level language.

# TYPES OF HIGH LEVEL LANGUAGES

As high level languages were developed to be application orientated rather than machine orientated, different applications have led to the development of different languages. The first high level languages to gain widespread use were in the scientific and technical areas. These were designed to enable formulae to be easily incorporated into programs. The best known of these languages is FORTRAN. Improvement in software design methods led to block structured languages, ALGOL was the first of these. Many of today's languages,

including Pascal, were developed from ALGOL. When computers started to be used for business applications, e.g. accounting and payroll, new languages were developed. The COBOL language gained wide acceptance in this area. In the 1970s and 1980s many laguages were developed for specialist applications particularly in the relational database field. These specialized languages designed for a particular application, sometimes called fourth generation languages (4GLs), are usually interpreted. Languages tailored for the needs of artificial intelligence and list processing have also been developed. These languages are quite different to the others and are often call non-procedural lanuages. Figure 3.6 summarizes the types of high level languages.

# HIGH LEVEL VERSUS LOW LEVEL LANGUAGES

For the majority of applications a suitable high level language can be chosen in which to program the solution. There are however a small number of occasions when a low level language solution is more appropriate.

Programs written in assembly language are generally more efficient in their use of CPU time than high level language equivalents. This is because even the most efficient, optimizing compilers tend to produce code which uses more instructions than that produced by a skilled assembly language programmer. The code produced by a compiler tends to make more use of main memory storage and less use of the CPU registers than an assembly language programmer would. Access time to main memory is slower than access to registers. So programs compiled from high level languages tend to run slower than assembly language programs.

Some programs, particularly in the real-time control environment, need access to special hardware attached to the CPU. The designers of high level languages have no knowledge of this specific hardware, so commands to use it are not included in the language. Programs written in assembly

| Language | Type | Applications |
|---|---|---|
| FORTRAN<br>COBOL | Unstructured | Scientific & technical<br>Business |
| ALGOL<br>Pascal<br>C<br>Ada<br>Modula2 | Block<br>structured | General purpose<br>Teaching & general purpose<br>Systems & general purpose<br>Military & high security<br>Real-time |
| BASIC | Simple | Simple introductory |
| C++<br>Small Talk | Object<br>orientated | General<br>purpose |
| Lisp<br>Prolog | Declarative | Artificial<br>intelligence |
| ORACLE<br>Ingres<br>SQL | 4GL | Relational<br>database |

**Figure 3.6** Some high level languages in common use.

language have access to the whole instruction set including any special instructions.

There are some situations where both the flexibility and rapid development time of a high level language, and the speed or direct access to hardware of low level programming is required. This is particularly true in the real time control world. For example, a program may be required to enable a user to control a piece of equipment. The user interface to the program is best written in a high level language, as writing screen handlers with windows and menus, etc., would be very difficult in assembly language. The part of the program which actually controls the hardware may need to be written in assembly language, perhaps to make use of the inherent speed of assembly language or maybe to access special hardware interfaces. The program is written as two modules, one in each language, then linked together by the linker. An alternative would be to write the majority of the program in a high level language, from which calls are made to library routines, which have been written in assembly language, to perform the time critical sections.

## Integrated development systems

Traditionally each of the tools required to create, translate and run a program were separate. The software developer used each tool in turn to produce the finished product.

In recent years there has been a trend with language system vendors to produce what are variously called "Integrated Development Environments" or "Programmer's Workbenches". In these systems all the tools required for program development, namely an editor, compiler, linker, and perhaps an assembler and a debug tool are integrated into one package. The analogy with a workbench is close; a mechanical engineer has a space on a bench upon which is placed his or her workpiece. Around the engineer, close to hand, are the various tools that may be needed. With a programmer's workbench the VDU screen is the space upon which the source text is displayed. Around the screen, usually in the form of menus or icons, are the various software tools such as editors, compilers, etc. Figures 3.7 and 3.8 show the working screen of two popular development environments.

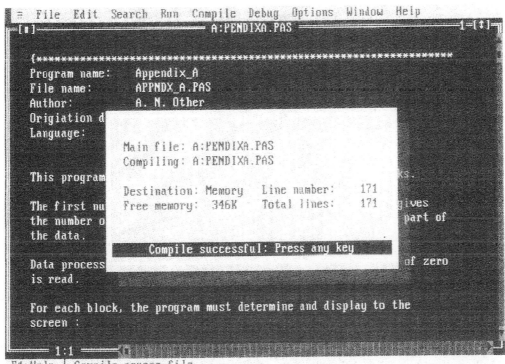

```
  Files  Edit  Compile  Link  Make  Run  Project  Options  Utilities  VID
 #1 C:\GALAXY\BOOK\PENDIXA.C                            Insert   Line 43   Col 1
  */

   input_block_length()

   {
     printf("\nPlease enter the next block indicator : ");
     scanf("%d",&block_length);
   }         Project: UNNAMED.PR
             Compiling ITOA.C            17
 /*********                                                               ***
   Set the b   Sizes = Code: 111, Const: 0, Data: 0
 */           No errors

   initialise_block()
 #2 C:\TB\SRC\C\ITOA.C                                  Insert   Line 1    Col 1
 /*
 ** itoa(n,s) - Convert n to characters in s
 */
 itoa(n, s) char *s; int n; {
   int sign;
   char *ptr;
```

Press CtrlBreak to abort

Figure 3.7

```
 =  File  Edit  Search  Run  Compile  Debug  Options  Window  Help
 [■]                          A:PENDIXA.PAS                            1-[↕]

   {*************************************************************************
   Program name:     Appendix_A
   File name:        APPNDX_A.PAS
   Author:           A. N. Other
   Origiation d
   Language:
                     Main file: A:PENDIXA.PAS
                     Compiling: A:PENDIXA.PAS
   This program                                                  ks.
                     Destination: Memory   Line number:    171
   The first nu      Free memory: 346K     Total lines:    171     gives
   the number o                                                      part of
   the data.
                     Compile successful: Press any key
   Data process                                                    of zero
   is read.

   For each block, the program must determine and display to the
   screen :

  1:1
 F1 Help | Compile source file
```

Figure 3.8

# SUMMARY

❑ Computers can only execute binary, machine code instructions.

❑ Machine code is difficult to use and understand; practical programs are written in assembly language or high level language.

❑ Assembly language is machine orientated, high level language is problem orientated.

❑ All programs have to be translated into machine code before they can be run.

# 4 Block structured languages

## INTRODUCTION

A software solution to a problem consists of two parts: code and data. The code is the list of instructions that need to be performed. The data are the pieces of information that are processed by the code. High level languages have means by which a programmer can specify in detail the code and data required for a particular problem.

## LANGUAGE STATEMENTS

Most high level languages are made up of statements. Some of these statements represent code, these are called executable statements. Other statements define the data, these are called data declaration statements.

### Executable statements

These represent the actions to be performed when the program is run. They consist of statements to carry out the primitive actions we met in Chapter 2, and also statements to control the sequence, selection and repetition of these primitives.

### Declaration statements

These give information to the compiler. The information is needed to enable it to translate the program correctly.

Pascal and C , the two languages we will be using, both separate executable statements and declaration statements. This separation of code and data enables programs to be produced that are easier to understand and much more reliable.

## KEYWORDS

High level languages use keywords or reserved words. These are words that are part of the language. They have a specific meaning to the compiler. Examples of keywords in C and Pascal are:

C

   while, if, int, switch

Pascal
   REPEAT, IF, WHILE, BEGIN

A complete list of keywords for C and Pascal is given in Appendix B.

As keywords are part of the language their meaning is fixed and cannot usually be redefined by the programmer.

## IDENTIFIERS

Identifiers are names chosen by the programmer to represent either items of data or sections of code. The programmer has a reasonably free choice for the names of identifiers. This is one aspect of high level languages that helps to make programs easier to understand.

There are some rules concerning the choice of identifiers. For C and Pascal these are:

- The name must begin with a letter.
- The first letter may be followed by any combination of letters, numbers and the underscore character "_".
- Spaces and punctuation, such as ; , . : ! and so on are not allowed.
- There may also be a limit on the length (in characters) of an identifier.

Examples of names that are allowed for identifiers

    temperature
    temperature1
    Pounds_and_pence
    Cash_total
    Get_input_values
    DisplayMenu
    side3_length

Examples of names that are not allowed for identifiers

| | |
|---|---|
| temperature one | (space not allowed) |
| 1temperature | (starts with a number) |
| Pounds&pence | (& not allowed) |
| Cash-total | ( - not allowed) |
| get.input.values | ( . not allowed) |
| error! | (! not allowed) |

The underscore character "_" can often be used to improve readability. Spaces are not allowed in identifiers, but omitting a space makes the name difficult to read. The underscore joins the two words but gives a natural break to the eye. From the examples above:

| | |
|---|---|
| Pounds and pence | not allowed |
| Poundsandpence | difficult to read |
| Pounds_and_pence | allowed and easier to read |

Care must be exercised when choosing names. In general the same name cannot be used to represent two different things. For example, a programmer may use the name "total" as an identifier for the sum of a list of numbers. The same name, "total", cannot be used as an identifier for the section of program that calculates the sum of the numbers.

In this case a better name would be, perhaps, "Calculate_Total".

In most languages identifier names cannot be the same as language keywords. For example in C and Pascal this means that the names "while", "if" and "else" are not acceptable as identifiers.

# VARIABLES

The concept of variables is fundamental to computer languages. A variable is a storage space for an item of data. Variables are allocated space in the computer's memory. In a program the space is referred to by using a name or identifier. The term variable is used to indicate that the value of the stored data may be changed. So the area of memory allocated to a variable may hold different values at different times.

## Data types

Each variable used in a program has associated with it a name and a type. The name is the identifier used by the programmer to refer to data stored in the variable. The type defines what kind of data is stored. The type of a variable is used by the compiler for two purposes. First it determines how much space in the computer's memory to allocate to the variable. Second it defines what kind of actions may be performed on the data. Data types fall into two broad categories: numeric and non-numeric. Numeric data types can be further divided into those that can only store whole numbers and those that may have decimal or fractional parts. This division into whole, or integer, numbers and non-integer numbers is necessary because of the way computers carry out arithmetic. Digital computers use binary arithmetic. Integer numbers can be represented in binary exactly. Non-integers however are represented in a way which may cause some loss of accuracy. Also the machine code instructions required, for example, to add two non-integers together are more complex than those required to add two integers together. For these reasons the compiler must know which type of numeric data is to be stored in a variable.

Non-integers are called floating point numbers. In general floating point variables are used to represent data that is measured. Integer variables are normally used to represent things that are counted.

The data type may also control the range of numbers which can be stored in variable. A compiler may allocate two bytes of storage for a particular integer data type. In this case only numbers in the range −32768 to 32767 can be stored. If four bytes are used then the range is −2147483648 to 2147483647.

Floating point variables take up more storage space. There are many methods available for storing floating point numbers in binary form. Each method is a compromise between storage space, range and accuracy. Some of the more common formats are shown in Fig. 4.1.

## Non-numeric data types

The commonest form of non-numeric data that is processed by computers is text. Text consists of characters. The normal set of characters includes the letters of the alphabet, upper and lower case; punctuation symbols, e.g. ", . ! ; other symbols, e.g. * & % $; and the numerals 0–9. A programmer may wish to store and process data of this type. Computers, however, can only store and process binary numbers. To overcome this problem each character within the character set is allocated a unique numeric code.

Various systems of character coding exist but by far the most popular is the American Standard Code for Information Interchange (ASCII).

Most high level languages have at least two different data types for storing textual information. The simplest is the character type. A variable of character type can hold one, and only one, character. The character may be any of the available set, letter, numeral or symbol. The character data type is rather limiting for the processing of larger amounts of text, e.g. sentences or commands. For these situations a string data type is used. A string is simply one or more characters stored together as a sequence. Clearly the actions that can be performed on variables holding textual information are very different from the actions performed on numeric data. Arithmetic on characters is not usually meaningful. Adding an ampersand (&) to a percent sign (%) has no meaning at all. There are some useful actions that can be carried out on text and we will meet these later on. Figure 4.2 illustrates how characters are stored and Fig. 4.3 shows how strings are stored.

## DATA DECLARATIONS

As we have seen above the compiler needs to know the type and name of each variable in a program before it can create any code to access the data in the variable. The programmer gives this information in a data declaration statement. A data declaration statement

| Format | Range | Accuracy significant digits | Size in bytes |
|---|---|---|---|
| IEEE | $1.2 \times 10^{-38}$ to $3.4 \times 10^{38}$ | 7 | 4 |
| Borland Pascal REAL | $2.9 \times 10^{-39}$ to $1.7 \times 10^{38}$ | 11 | 6 |
| DEC VAX | $5.6 \times 10^{-309}$ to $9.0 \times 10^{307}$ | 15 | 8 |

**Figure 4.1** Floating point number formats.

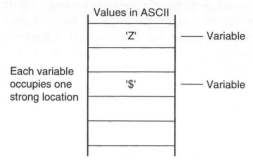

Figure 4.2 Storage of characters.

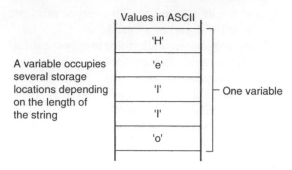

Figure 4.3 Storage of strings

is needed to associate a name and a data type for each variable. The data declaration must occur in the program **before** any reference to the variable.

## Data declarations in PASCAL

The general form of the data declaration statement is:

VAR <identifier list> : <data type> ;

The <identifier list> is a list of identifier names separated by commas. The data type is the type to be given to the identifiers in the list. Pascal has several inherent data types plus the ability to create user defined types (see Chapter 11). The inherent data types are:

| | |
|---|---|
| INTEGER | Whole numbers |
| REAL | Floating point numbers |
| CHAR | Single characters |
| BOOLEAN | TRUE or FALSE |

Some implementations of Pascal also support

| | |
|---|---|
| STRING | Sequence of characters |
| LongInt | Whole numbers with larger range |
| LongReal | Floating point numbers with larger range |
| WORD | Unsigned whole numbers |

To declare two variables holding data on the temperature and pressure of a gas we could use.

```
VAR  temperature,
     pressure : REAL;
```

A variable to store the single letter reply to a question could be declared thus:

```
VAR  reply : CHAR;
```

If several declarations are required the keyword VAR need only be used once.

```
VAR  Maths_mark,
     Science_mark,
     Average_mark : REAL;
     No_of_students,
     No_of_passes,
     No_of_fails  : INTEGER;
```

The above declares three real variables and three integer variables.

## Data declarations in C

The general form of the data declaration statement is

<data type> <identifier list> ;

The <identifier list> is a list of identifier names separated by commas. The data type is the type to be given to the identifiers in the list. C has several inherent data types plus the ability to create user defined types (see Chapter 11). The inherent data types are:

| | |
|---|---|
| int | Whole numbers |
| float | Floating point numbers |
| char | Single characters |

| long | Whole numbers with larger range |
|------|---------------------------------|
| double | Floating point number with larger range |

The data types int, char and long may be pre-fixed with "unsigned" if positive only values are needed.

To declare two variables holding data on the temperature and pressure of a gas we could use

```
float temperature,
        pressure;
```

A variable to store the single letter reply to a question could be declared thus:

```
char    reply;
```

The following declares three floating point variables and three integer variables

```
float    Maths_mark,
         Science_mark,
         Average_mark;
int      No_of_students,
         No_of_passes,
         No_of_fails;
```

## Declarations of character strings

Programmers use two different types of string data. The simplest is literal strings. A literal string is a sequence of characters which is written in to the program. A literal string is fixed when the program is compiled and cannot change when the program is run. Literal strings are used mainly for the display of messages on an output device. In most languages literal strings are denoted by the use of either single or double quote marks. For example

"This is a literal string"

The second type of string data is string variables. As we saw above strings are stored with each character in consecutive memory locations. So the amount of memory space required for a string depends on its size. Generally this is not so for numeric data, the integer values 4 and 4000 occupy the same amount of memory space. Previously we saw

that one purpose of data types is to inform the compiler how much memory is required for a variable. So when string variables are declared a value representing the size is required. This value is the maximum length of string which can be stored in the variable. The actual length of the string may be less than this.

## String declarations in C

The length of the string is given in square brackets after the variable name. The following declares a string called "message" to hold a maximum of 25 characters.

```
char     message[25];
```

## String declarations in Pascal

The ISO Pascal language definition does not include a string data type. However, many modern implementations of the language include one as an extension. The most common type is called STRING. Using this as an example, the following declares a string called "message" to hold a maximum of 25 characters.

```
VAR message : STRING[25];
```

If your compiler does not support STRING then you may need to use "PACKED ARRAY OF CHAR". Check with your compiler documentation.

## BLOCKS AND COMPOUND STATEMENTS

As we have seen, programs consist of primitive actions and functions to control the order in which these primitives are carried out. Frequently these actions form logical groups. Also we frequently find that a group of actions can be treated *en bloc*. That is if one action is to be repeated, then the group as a whole has to be repeated. Similarly if one action is to be selected, or not selected, then the whole group should be treated likewise. It is as if the group of statements are glued together and must be treated as one unit. Block structured languages formalize this by allowing the programmer to define blocks, also called compound statements. A block is a group of simple statements. Between each statement there is a separator. In both C and Pascal the separator is a semicolon ";".

In Pascal the keyword BEGIN denotes the start of a block. The keyword END denotes the end. The open and close brace (or curly bracket) characters "{" and "}" are used in C to show the begining and end of a block.

The use of compound statements, or blocks, is hierarchical. A block consists of a group of simple statements, but any simple statement may be replaced with a block. Therefore we can have blocks within blocks within blocks, etc. This ties in with our top down design principle. The top level block is divided into lower level blocks. At each level more detail is added, until the lowest, primitive, actions are performed by simple statements.

## PUTTING COMMENTS IN PROGRAMS

High level languages like C and Pascal look similar to English. Programs written in these languages should be reasonably easy to read. The program statements tell a reader what actions are taken when the program is run. What it is not always clear is why the program takes these actions. Also complex sections of code may be difficult to follow. This may be particularly so for someone other than the programmer. To help explain the program it is helpful to put comments into the source code.

Comments are sections of text which are readable by humans but totally ignored by the compiler. Comments should be added anywhere in a program where confusion could arise. Each major section of a program requires a comment explaining its purpose.

The method of inserting comments in a program varies from language to language. Most languages have a character or sequence of characters said to "open" a comment. Another character, or sequence, is used to "close" a comment. All text between the open and close characters is ignored by the compiler.

To open a comment in Pascal a programmer uses the sequence "(*". To close the comment the sequence "*)" is used. Some Pascal compilers permit an alternative using the brace (or curly bracket) characters "{ }"

A comment in C is opened by the two character sequence /*, the comment is closed with the reverse sequence */.

Comments may spread across several lines of text, or may be just a few words following a program statement.

Examples of comments in Pascal and C

```
{This program converts a measure-
ment in feet and inches to metres
and millimetres}
cm_per_inch; (*conversion factor*)
= 2*pi*frequency*capacitance; /*
calculate the impedance*/
```

## SUMMARY

❑ Programs written in a high level language consist of statements;

❑ There are two different type of statement; declaration statements and executable statements.

❑ Each item of data that is declared has an associated data type.

❑ Block structured languages group statements into blocks.

# EXERCISES

1.  Which of the following Boolean expressions equates to **false**

    |         | Pascal          | C            |
    |---------|-----------------|--------------|
    | (a)     | 6 <> 8–2        | 6 != 8–2     |
    | (b)     | 'a' = 'A''      | a' == 'A'    |
    | (c)     | 7516 <= 7516    | 7516 <= 7516 |
    | (d)     | 937 >= 29       | 937 >= 29    |

2.1. Which of the Pascal data types, **integer, real, boolean** and **char** could be used for each of the values below?

   (a)  167
   (b)  56.9
   (c)  –49
   (d)  FALSE
   (e)  '7'

2.2. Which of the C data types int, float and char could be used for each of the values below?

   (a)  167
   (b)  56.9
   (c)  –49
   (d)  0
   (e)  '7'

3.  A certain program requires three variables to hold data for:

    A salesmans name,
    the number of items sold in a week,
    the total weekly value of sales by the salesman.

    In your chosen language show variable declarations for these variables, and explain your choice of data types.

# 5 Simple programs

## INTRODUCTION

In the last chapter we saw how programs are made up of declaration statements and executable statements. We saw in Chapter 2 how a task could be broken up into smaller tasks. In this chapter we are going to match up the required tasks with program statements.

## SIMPLE PROGRAMS

Many simple programs follow a basic pattern.

1. Obtain some input
2. Perform some calculations
3. Produce some output.

For our first steps in writing a program we will take these separately. Programs consisting of only stage 1 or stage 2 are not realistic, nor can they be tested properly, so we will start with stage 3.

## PRODUCING OUTPUT

Output from a program can take many forms. Program output is a form of communication. It usually consists of sending data to a computer peripheral. The peripheral then converts this data into a signal of the appropriate form. The signal may be designed to be received by a person or another machine. We will concentrate on output intended for human consumption. The output could be visual, perhaps on a VDU or printer, or a flashing lamp. It could be audible, anything from a simple beep to a recognizable tune. Or it could involve movement, e.g. a robot arm. Some of these are obviously very specific to a particular application. For general-purpose output most computer systems provide a character-based display. It is this form of output we will use.

The simplest output only type of programs are those which display a message. Perhaps we want to display the following:

> This is my first program

The programs to achieve this in C and Pascal are shown in Figs 5.1 and 5.2.
Both programs follow the same basic pattern. First there is a header followed by a block.

### The "First" C program

For this basic program the header is very simple. It is the line

```
#include <stdio.h>
```

This tells the compiler that the program makes use of the standard input–output functions.

Next comes the block. The block is a function called "main". A C program may have many functions, but the function "main" is always where the program starts. (We will see how to create other functions in Chapter 6.)

The opening brace ({) indicates the start of a block. The closing brace (}) denotes the end

```
#include <stdio.h>
main()
{
printf("This is my first program\n");
}
```

**Figure 5.1** Output only program in C.

```
PROGRAM First(INPUT,OUTPUT);
BEGIN
WRITELN('This is my first program');
END.
```

**Figure 5.2** Output only program in Pascal.

of the block. Only one statement makes up the block. It is the line beginning printf. The `printf` function performs formatted output. The output in this case is a simple string of characters followed by a new line character. Double quote marks (") are used to enclose the string of characters. The character sequence (\n) denotes a new line. The `printf` function can format and output a wide variety of data. Some of these facilities we will meet later.

### The "First" Pascal program

The Pascal program's header is the statement

```
PROGRAM First(INPUT,OUTPUT);
```

This tells the compiler that the program is called "First" and makes use of the standard input–output devices.

Next comes the block. The start of the block is indicated by the keyword BEGIN The keyword END denotes the end of the block. Only one statement makes up the block. It is the line beginning WRITELN. The WRITELN (pronounced WRITE LiNe) statement displays one line of formatted output. In this case the output consists of a string of characters. The characters to be displayed are enclosed within single quote marks ('). WRITELN is used to output a wide variety of data. Some of which we will meet later.

## OBTAINING INPUT

When a program obtains some input data it does so by communicating with a peripheral device. This device may be under human control, e.g. a keyboard or a mouse. Other peripheral devices may provide data read from a machine, e.g. a modem or a magnetic tape. Most general-purpose computer systems provide a keyboard for character input. It is this form of input we will discuss first.

When data are obtained from outside a program and read into the program they must be stored somewhere internally. We saw in the last chapter that high level languages use variables for storage space. So in any program that obtains input data there must be at least one variable. Therefore our first program to use input data will also be our first program to use a data declaration.

As an example of a simple program combining both input and output we will use the following:

■ A program to read an integer value from the keyboard, and then display the value with a message.

■ A design for the program is a simple sequence of three actions.

1. Output a prompt message.
2. Obtain some data from the keyboard.
3. Output a message and the data.

The programs to achieve this in C and Pascal are shown in Figs 5.3 and 5.4.

## The simple input–output program in C

For this program the header is similar to the previous program. The difference being the variable declaration. The statement

```
int a_number;
```

declares an integer variable called a_number.

The function main has three statements. The first statement uses printf to display a message prompting the user to type a number. Note that we have not used the \n sequence to give a new line. Therefore the keyboard input will appear on the same line as the prompt message.

The next statement uses the scanf function. This function is used to scan an input line according to a given format. The format is given in the string "%d". The % means the next letter specifies a format, the "d" specifies a decimal number. We will meet other format specifers later. The format string is followed by the variable into which the input data is to be stored, in this case a_number. Note that the variable name is preceded by an ampersand (&). The significance of the ampersand will be explained in Chapter 11.

The last statement of the block is another printf. The string in quotes is The number was %d\n.

The first three words will be displayed. But the %d will be replaced with the decimal representation of the value stored in the variable following the format string, in this case a_number.

## The simple input–output program in Pascal

The header is similar to the previous program

```
#include <stdio.h>
int a_number;
main()
{
printf("Please input the number ");
scanf("%d",&a_number);
printf("The number was %d\n",a_number);
}
```

**Figure 5.3** Input and output program in C.

```
PROGRAM Second(INPUT,OUTPUT);
VAR a_number : INTEGER;
BEGIN
WRITE('Please input the number ');
READLN(a_number);
WRITELN('The number was ',a_number);
END.
```

**Figure 5.4** Simple input–output program in Pascal.

with the addition of the data declaration. An integer variable is declared with the statement :

```
VAR a_number : INTEGER;
```

The main body of the program consists of three statements. The first statement uses WRITE to display a message prompting the user to type a number. Note the use of WRITE rather than WRITELN. This enables the users input to appear on the same line as the prompt message.

The next statement uses READLN to read a line of data from the keyboard. The data is read and then stored in the variable given in brackets after READLN, in this case a_number.

The last statement uses WRITELN to display the string given in quotes, i.e. The number was, followed by the decimal representation of the value stored in the variable a_number. The variable name is not enclosed in quotes. This denotes that it is the value stored in a_number and not the word a_number itself which is to be displayed.

## Program operation

When the program is run the prompt message is displayed. All requests for information from a user should be preceded by a prompt message. The user cannot be expected to guess what data is required. Then the program waits for the user to type the input data. The user indicates the input data is complete by pressing the <ENTER> (or <RETURN>) key. The inputted data is then stored in the designated variable and the program continues to the next statement. This statement displays the second message followed by the decimal representation of the value stored in the variable.

The data is input and displayed as a decimal number made up of a series of characters, but it is important to remember that internal to the program the value is stored in binary. Therefore the input and output routines convert from decimal to binary on input, and from binary to decimal on output.

## Inputting strings of characters

We have seen how to output character strings and numeric data. We have also read numeric data into a program. There are often circumstances when a program needs to obtain non-numeric, i.e. character-based, data. As with numeric input a variable must be declared to hold the data.

As we saw in Chapter 4, to declare a string variable the maximum length of the input character string must be known. At the time the program is written it is not possible to know this. The programmer has no control over how much the user will type when the program is run. For simple programs we make an assumption about the maximum string length. Fully developed professional programs check the number of characters typed against the maximum, but we will leave that for later.

Modifying the numeric input program for character input gives us:

1. Output a prompt message.
2. Obtain a character string from the keyboard.
3. Output a message and the string.

The programs to achieve this in C and Pascal are shown in Figs 5.5 and 5.6.

These programs are similar to those of Figs 5.3 and 5.4. The string variable is declared as name with a maximum length of 20 characters. In the C program the format specifier %s is used instead of %d. Pascal determines the format from the data type, so there is very little difference between programs 5.4 and 5.6.

In Chapter 2 we saw that all programs are made up of just four primitives. Recall that these were

1. Input data from the outside world.
2. Output data to the outside world.
3. Move data from one storage area to another.
4. Perform a simple one-step calculation.

We have produced simple programs involving the first and second primitives. With most high level languages the third and fourth

```
#include <stdio.h>
char name[20];
main()
{
printf("What is your name ? ");
scanf("%s",name);
printf("Hello %s\n",name);
}
```

**Figure 5.5** Character string input program in C.

```
PROGRAM Third(INPUT,OUTPUT);
VAR name : STRING[20];
BEGIN
WRITE('What is your name ? ');
READLN(name);
WRITELN('Hello ',name);
END.
```

**Figure 5.6** Character string input program in Pascal.

primitives are accomplished using the same mechanism. This is the assignment statement.

## ASSIGNMENT STATEMENT

The assignment statement is used to assign some value to a variable. The value is stored in the variable. It replaces any value that was previously stored there. The value is determined by evaluating an expression. Expressions can be very complex, but are essentially similar to mathematical algebraic formulae.

The simplest expressions consist of only one term. This may be a constant or a variable. Assignment statements of this kind are used to implement the third primitive, moving data. The variable being assigned to is on the left-hand side of an assignment symbol and the data to be assigned is on the right. So, if the assignment symbol is ← we have;

$$variable \leftarrow data$$

To move a known, fixed value into a variable an assignment of the form

$$variable \leftarrow constant$$

is used. To move a unknown value into a variable from another variable an assignment of the form

$$variable1 \leftarrow variable2$$

is used.

The assignment symbol in Pascal is the two character sequence ":=". The assignment symbol in C is the = character. In both cases the equals sign is used. It is important not to confuse assignment with mathematical equality. To separate assignment from equality it helps if the assignment symbol is pronounced as becomes, or is assigned. So the C statement

$$pressure = 57;$$

should be pronounced

"pressure becomes 57"

or

"pressure is assigned 57"

Equality represents a state of being, that is one thing is (already) equal to another. Assignment represents an action, that is make one thing equal to another.

Figures 5.7 and 5.8 give examples of simple assignment statements in C and Pascal, respectively. It can be assumed that the variables have all been declared with suitable data types.

## CALCULATIONS

The assignment statement is also used when a new value needs to be calculated by performing arithmetic operations on existing data. The required operations are contained in an expression. In most computer languages expressions are written in a manner similar to algebraic formulae. In its simplest form an expression consists of two variables or constants separated by an operator. The usual four arithmetic operators, plus, subtract, multiply and divide are available together

```
pressure = 57;
temperature = 21.6;
new_value = old_value;
response = "The answer is ";
letter = 'Q';
```

**Figure 5.7** Simple assignment statements in C.

```
pressure := 57;
temperature := 21.6;
new_value := old_value;
response := 'The answer is ';
letter := 'Q';
```

**Figure 5.8** Simple assignment statements in Pascal.

with more specialized ones depending on the language. For more complex calculations several operators may be used. Each one is separated from the next by a variable or constant. The order in which the operations are carried out is the same as that for arithmetic. Division and multiplication are performed before addition and subtraction. Brackets (parentheses) are used to enforce a different order.

Examples of simple expressions

```
5.8 + 78.2
pressure / volume
0.5 * base * height
2 * PI * radius
(cost + mark_up) * VAT_rate
```

Note, most computer languages use * and / to represent multiply and divide, respectively. Combining expressions with assignment statements gives the capability of calculating new data. Figures 5.9 and 5.10 show this in C and Pascal.

## ASSIGNMENT COMPATIBILITY

It is important that the type of data formed by the expression on the right-hand side of an assignment is compatible with the data

```
volume = length*width*height;
net_pay=hours*rate-deductions;
celcius=(farenheit-32)*5/9;
```

**Figure 5.9** Examples of calculations in C.

```
volume:=length*width*height;
net_pay:=hours*rate-deductions;
celcius:=(farenheit-32)*5 /9;
```

**Figure 5.10** Examples of calculations in Pascal.

type of the variable on the left-hand side. In general, if any of the variables or constants on the right-hand side are floating point then the variable on the left-hand side must be a floating point type. If all the variables and constants in the expression are integers the left-hand variable can be an integer type, providing the expression contains no division. This is because addition, subtraction or multiplication of two integers always yields an integer value. Division of two integers may give an integer result, but it may not depending on the two numbers concerned. For example the integer 10 divided by the integer 8 gives the non-integer result 1.25. Because of this problem computer languages have two types of division, integer division and floating point division.

### Integer versus floating point division

Floating point division produces the usual expected quotient when any number is divided by any other. The result is a floating point number as close as possible to the actual quotient. Integer division does not correspond to division as in "normal" arithmetic. The result of integer division is an integer ignoring any fractional part or remainder. The remainder (or modulus) can be be obtained by a special operator. Some examples may make this clearer and are given in the table at the top of the next page.

| Floating point division | Integer division | Integer modulus |
|---|---|---|
| 10/2 = 5.0 | 10/2 = 5 | 10 mod  2 = 0 |
| 16.0/4.0 = 4.0 | 16/4 = 4 | 16 mod  4 = 0 |
| 10/8 = 1.25 | 10/8 = 1 | 10 mod  4 = 2 |
| 48/13 = 3.692308 | 48/13 = 3 | 48 mod 13 = 9 |

Pascal uses the keyword DIV to denote integer division and MOD for the modulus operator. C uses the same symbol (/) for both integer and floating point division. Which type of division is performed depends on the data types of the dividend and divisor. If either the dividend or divisor are floating point numbers then floating point division is performed, otherwise integer division is performed. If both terms on the right-hand side are integers then integer division is performed even though the variable on the left-hand side may be of type float. This can sometimes cause confusion.

## Assigning integer values to floating variables

Being assignment compatible does not always mean the data types of the right- and left-hand sides of an assignment are the same. It is permissible to assign an integer expression on the right-hand side to a floating point variable on the left-hand side. It is important to note that this results in the integer number being converted to its equivalent floating point value which may result in loss of accuracy in later calculations as discussed in Chapter 4.

## INPUT–CALCULATE–OUTPUT PROGRAMS

We saw in Chapter 2 that many simple problems can be broken down into three stages, obtain the data, calculate the answer, display the output. We can now take the weight conversion problem from Chapter 2 and write a program to meet our design. The C and Pascal solutions are given in Figs 5.11 and 5.12,

```c
#include <stdio.h>
int pounds,
ounces; /* Pounds and ounces values are whole numbers */
float kilos; /* Kilos value will have fractional part */
main()
{
/* Prompt for and obtain the input data */
printf("Please enter the pounds\n");
scanf("%d",&pounds);
printf("Please enter the ounces\n");
scanf("%d",&ounces);
/* Convert to ounces then to kilos */
ounces = pounds * 16 + ounces;
kilos = ounces / 35.2;
/* Display the result */
printf("The weight in kilos is ");
printf("%f\n",kilos);
}
```

Figure 5.11 The weight conversion program in C.

```
PROGRAM Weight(INPUT,OUTPUT);
VAR pounds,
ounces : INTEGER; {Pounds and ounces values are whole numbers} ≥
kilos : REAL; { Kilos will have fractional part }≥
BEGIN
{ Prompt for and obtain the input data }
  WRITELN('Please enter the pounds');
  READLN(pounds);
  WRITELN('Please enter the ounces');
  READLN(ounces);
  { Convert to ounces then to kilos }
  ounces := pounds * 16 + ounces;
  kilos := ounces / 35.2;
  { Display the result }
  WRITE('The weight in kilos is');
  WRITELN(kilos);
  END.
```

**Figure 5.12** The weight conversion program in Pascal.

respectively. Note the use of comments to break the programs into their logical sections.

## OUTPUT FORMAT OF FLOATING POINT NUMBERS

When displaying floating point values on an output device it is usually desirable to specify the format of the output. Floating point numbers may be displayed in scientific (or exponential) format or in conventional format. In science and engineering it is common to express numbers in the form $2.347 \times 10^2$. The same number in conventional format is 234.7. Scientific format is useful for very large or very small numbers as it eliminates the need for the many zeros required in conventional format. As most computer displays cannot handle the superscript notation, a modified form is used. This displays an "E", for Exponent, instead. So the number above is displayed as 2.347E+02 The plus sign is replaced with a minus sign for numbers less than one, e.g. 0.00789 will be displayed as 7.89E–03.

If conventional format is preferred the number of decimal places may be specified. In this case the number is automatically rounded up or down to the specified number of digits. It is important to remember that this rounding only occurs on the display, the value stored in the variable is unaffected.

### Output formatting in C

The format specifiers used with `printf` are very flexible and allow a good control of the output format. The specifier `%f` is used for conventional format, the `%e` specifier is used to give scientific format. The number of decimal places and leading or trailing zeros can also be controlled. Also left or right justification and other features are supported. Consult your compiler documentation for details.

### Output formatting in Pascal

The default format produced by `WRITELN` is scientific. If conventional format is required then a field width specifier must be used. This immediately follows the variable name in the `WRITELN` statement. It has the general form :<total width>:<decimal place>. So in the following statement the value of metres_per_mile will be displayed in nine character spaces with two decimal places.

WRITELN
('There are',metres_per_mile:9:2, metres in a mile');

The resulting output would look like:

There are 1609.34 metres in a mile

If the total width specifier is too small then the whole number will be displayed but with no leading spaces. Numbers are always right justified within the specified width.

## SUMMARY

❑ Programs perform output to the user with the WRITELN or printf statements.

❑ Input data can be received from the user with the READLN or scanf statements.

❑ Movement of data and calculations are both achieved using an assignment statement.

❑ Conventional algebraic type notation is used for assignment expressions.

## EXERCISES

1. Write a program to read two whole numbers from the keyboard and then display them in reverse order, i.e. the second one first.
2. Write a program to read in a string then display the string three times on one line. For example if the user types "Cheers" the program should display "CheersCheersCheers".
3. Write a program in your chosen language to implement the following:

   Set a first variable to 20 and a second variable to 30.
   Display the values of both variables.
   Read a value from the keyboard into the first variable.
   Copy the value from the first variable to the second variable.
   Display both variables.

4. Design and write a program to read a number and then display the square and cube of the number.
5. Design and write a program to calculate the average value of four numbers typed at the keyboard.
6. Design and write a program to read a floating point number representing a length in metres. The program should then display the equivalent length in feet and inches to the nearest whole inch.
7. The boiling point of water reduces by approximately 1°C for each 300 metres altitude above sea level. Design and write a program to calculate the boiling point at an altitude entered from the keyboard.
8. Given two internal angles of a triangle write a program to calculate the third angle.

# 6 Modular programming

## INTRODUCTION

In Chapter 2 we used the top down technique of modularization and stepwise refinement to divide a problem into smaller problems. Modern, block structured, languages like Pascal and C have a means of dividing the code into smaller sections. This has all the advantages of modularization as discussed in Chapter 2, plus added benefits derived from modular code.

## MODULAR PROGRAMMING

Large software projects usually have a team of programmers all working on the solution. If the programs are produced in a modular fashion each programmer can work on one or more modules separately. With a large, complex problem it is difficult for one person to understand the whole task and, at the same time, deal with the minute coding detail of a small section. With each programmer working on a more manageable sized task the work can be divided among the team more effectively. Even for smaller programs, produced by only one programmer, modularization has advantages. Modular programs are easier to read and understand. Those only needing an overview of the program's functions can concentrate on the top level modules. Someone needing a more detailed knowledge of the program can study the lower level modules. This makes the program easier to maintain. Maintainability is improved for other reasons: updating or modifying a modular program is made easier. Often a module can simply be replaced by a newer version. Finding errors in modular programs is made easier, usually each module is tested separately. This way the testing is concentrated on a small section of code at any one time.

## IMPLEMENTING MODULES

In block structured languages each section, or module, is called a block. In Pascal the sections are called procedures, in C they are called functions (see Figs 6.1 and 6.2 for an example in each language). In both languages each section consists of a header declaration and a statement block called the body. We saw in Chapter 4 that a data declaration is used to associate a name with a storage location. A procedure declaration has a similar purpose. It associates a name with a section of code. Just as we refer to data storage by name so we can refer to a section of code by name.

The language statements that make up the section are only translated once into machine code by the compiler. However, we may cause the code to be executed many times simply by referring to the code section by name. This is known as calling the procedure or function.

```
PROCEDURE Firstone; <= Pascal procedure declaration
BEGIN
.
.   Statements making up the body
.   of the procedure go in here
.
END;
```

**Figure 6.1** A skeleton Pascal procedure.

```
firstone()    ← C function declaration
{
.
.   Statements making up the body
.   of the function go in here
.
}
```

**Figure 6.2** A skeleton C function.

For Pascal . . . Firstone;...

For C

```
    .
    .
    firstone();
    .
    .
```

When a procedure or function is "called" control transfers to its first executable statement. The statements in the body are then executed. When the last statement has been executed control returns to the point from which the procedure was called.

A procedure (or function) may be called many times in a program, though it must only be declared once. Each time it is called the statements in its body are carried out. So where a call is made to a procedure or function it is as though the statements making up

the body are inserted at that point in the program.

In Chapter 2 we designed a program to convert from pounds and ounces to kilograms. In the last chapter we wrote this program as a single block. We can now write

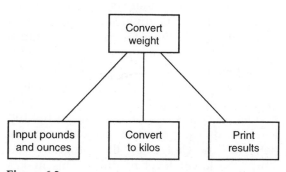

**Figure 6.3.**

```
PROGRAM Weight (INPUT, OUTPUT);
VAR pounds,
     ounces      :INTEGER;
     kilos :REAL;
PROCEDURE Getweight;
BEGIN
     WRITELN ('Please enter the pounds');
     READLN (pounds);
     WRITELN ('Please enter the ounces');
     READLN (ounces);
END;
PROCEDURE Convert-to-kilos;
BEGIN
     ounces:=pounds*16+ounces;
     kilos:=ounces/35.2;
END;
PROCEDURE Results;
BEGIN
     WRITELN ('The weight in kilos is');
     WRITELN (kilos);
END;
BEGIN
     Getweight;
     Convert-to-kilos;
     Results;
END.
```

**Figure 6.4** The modularized weight conversion program in Pascal.

the modularized program from the design in Chapter 2 (see Fig. 6.3).

We can see there are four sections: a main module, an input module, a calculation module and an output module. We now convert these to functions or procedures. The actual statements required to carry out the operations are the same as the programs in Figs 5.11 and 5.12. The only difference is in the structure of the program and not in method used to solve the problem.

If we compare the modularized programs in Figs 6.4 and 6.5 with those of Chapter 2, we see the new versions are longer and appear to be more complex. Modularization was supposed to make our programs easier. Why are they more complicated? The reason is

because this is a fairly simple example. The whole program was small enough to understand as one unit, without subdividing it into modules. Larger programs cannot easily be understood as a whole. As we develop more complex programs the advantages of modularization will become more obvious.

# ORDER OF PROCEDURE DECLARATIONS

In general we must have declared a procedure, or function, before we can call it. In Pascal this means that all the procedure declarations must come before the main block. With C the situation is not as simple. In earlier versions of C there was no restriction on

```
#include <stdio.h>
int    pounds,
       ounces;
float  kilos;
main()
       {
       getweight();
       convert-to-kilos();
       results();
       }
getweight()
       {
       printf ("Please enter the pounds\n");
       scanf("%d",&pounds);
       printf("Please enter the ounces\n");
       scanf("%d",&ounces);
       }
convert_to_kilos()
       {
       ounces = pounds * 16 + ounces;
       kilos = ounces / 35.2;
results()
       {
       printf("The weight in kilos is\n");
       printf("%f\n",kilos);
```

**Figure 6.5** The modularized weight conversion program in C.

calling a function that had not yet been declared. It became conventional to put the main function first followed by the lower level functions. However the latest ANSI C specification requires functions to be declared before they are called. This has led to the introduction of function prototypes. A prototype is basically the header part of the declaration without the statement body. Consult your compiler documentation to check if it accepts prototypes. The rest of the example programs in this book will include prototypes, omit them if your compiler does not support them.

# EXERCISES

1. Write a modular program to convert a temperature in Celsius to the equivalent in Fahrenheit and Kelvin.
2. Write a modular version of your solution to Exercise 5.6.
3. Give four advantages of modular programming.

# 7 Selection and iteration

## CONDITIONAL STATEMENTS

To implement the selection parts of a design we use conditional statements. A conditional statement tests some condition and then performs an action depending on the truth, or otherwise, of the condition. In most languages this is known as the "if" statement. It is generally of the form:

if condition is true then perform action.

If the condition is true then the action is performed. If the condition is not true the action is not performed. The meaning is similar to the "if" we met in pseudocode in Chapter 2. The condition is an expression which can have one of only two values, **true** or **false**. Most conditional expressions rely on comparisons. In assignment expressions we use operators such as plus and minus. In conditional expressions we use comparison operators, e.g. equal to or less than. There are six comparison operators:

- Equal to
- Not equal to
- Greater than
- Greater than or equal to
- Less than
- Less than or equal to.

Figure 7.1 shows the symbols used in C and Pascal.

A conditional expression may contain variables, constants and conditional operators. If a variable is used then the condition will be true or false depending on the value of the variable when the condition is evaluated. Arithmetic expressions may also be used in a conditional expression. The expression is evaluated and the resulting value used in the comparison. Figure 7.2 shows some examples.

## PRACTICAL IF STATEMENTS

The syntax of the if statement differs slightly between C and Pascal.

C uses the form:

        if (condition) statement;

Pascal uses the form:

        IF condition THEN statement;

| Operator | C symbol | Pascal symbol |
|---|---|---|
| Equal to | == | = |
| Not equal to | != | <> |
| Greater than | > | > |
| Greater than or equal to | >= | >= |
| Less than or equal to | <= | <= |

**Figure 7.1** Conditional operators in C and Pascal.

| Expression | Value |
|---|---|
| 6 < 7 | true |
| 6 >= 7 | false |
| number = number + 1 | false |
| −8 < 2 | true |
| a ! = a | false |
| 6 = 12 / 2 | true |
| 8 + 2 − 1 > 3 * 4 | false |

**Figure 7.2** Conditional expressions.

In both cases the statement is only executed if the condition is true. If the condition is false, execution continues with the next statement. If more than one statement is dependent upon the condition then the simple statement is replaced with a compound statement or block. Figures 7.3 and 7.4 show examples of if statements.

The simple if statement allows a selection between executing a statement or not executing it. For a two-way selection we add an else clause to the if statement. Thus the if with an else becomes:

For C

> if ( condition ) statement 1;
> else statement 2;

For Pascal

> IF condition THEN statement 1
>     ELSE statement 2;

```
IF voltage>limit THEN WRITELN('Warning');

IF month = 6 THEN month_name:='July';

IF hours + 1 = 13 THEN hours:= 1;

IF week_number = 3 THEN
     IF day = 5 THEN Pay_day;

IF number MOD 2 = 1 THEN
     BEGIN
          odds := odds + 1;
          WRITELN(number,' is odd');
     END;
```

**Figure 7.3** Examples of Pascal IF statements.

```
if (voltage > limit) printf("Warning\n");

if (month == 6) month_name = "July";

if (hours +1 == 13) hours = 1;

if (week_number == 3)
     if (day == 5) pay_day();

if (number %2==1)
     {
          odds = odds + 1;
          printf("%d is odd",number);
     }
```

**Figure 7.4** Examples of C if statements.

In both cases statement 1 is executed if the condition is true and statement 2 is executed if it is false.

## Boolean values

The Pascal language has a data type BOOLEAN. Variables may be declared to be of type BOOLEAN and have values assigned to them. These values may only be true or false. If "test" has been declared to be a BOOLEAN variable then the following assignment statement is allowable

```
test := speed > maximum_speed;
```

The variable "test" will hold the value true or false. Later in the program a statement of the form

```
IF test THEN WRITELN('Speed limit
exceeded !');
```

could be used. In Pascal conditional expressions may only be assigned to BOOLEAN variables. C does not have a Boolean data type. Boolean values may be stored in integer variables. The ANSI C specification states that zero is to be taken as false and any other value as true. In practice most compilers use one to represent true, but this cannot be relied upon as some compilers use minus one. The example above written in C becomes:

```
int test ;
test = speed > maximum_speed;
if ( test ) printf("Speed limit
exceeded !\n");
```

Assignment expressions in C have a value. The value of the expression is the same as the value actually assigned. This allows statements such as:

```
x = y = z + 7;
```

In this case the value of "z + 7" is assigned to "y" and the value of that expression is assigned to "x". The result is to assign the same value to "x" and "y". Because an integer value can be considered "true" or "false" and an assignment has a value then an assignment can be "true" or "false". This leads to statements similar to

```
if ( pressure = read_pressure() )
```

This statement assigns to "pressure" the value returned from the function "read_pressure" then, if the assigned value is non-zero the rest of the statement is executed. In this way an assignment and a selection can be made in the same statement. This technique has its dangers. Consider the following statements

```
if ( count - 25 ) printf(" count
is 25\n");
else printf(" count is not 25\n");
```

It would seem reasonably logical, albeit rather pointless. In fact the result of the above statements is to display "count is 25" regardless of the value of "count". The value of the expression "count = 25" is 25 and therefore "true", so the else part will never be executed. Also "count" will be assigned the value of 25 which was probably not intended. The correct syntax is:

```
if ( count == 25 ) printf(" count
is 25\n");
else printf(" count is not 25\n");
```

One way to avoid this trap is when determining the equality of a variable and a constant, always put the constant first. This way the compiler will detect a syntax error if = rather than == is used.

```
if ( 25 = count )   ← Syntax error

if ( count = 25 )   ← Correct syntax
```

but wrong logic

## BOOLEAN OPERATORS

The "if" statements we have met so far have involved only one condition being either "true" or "false". In real situations a selection may rely on either of two (or more) conditions being true. Or sometimes we may wish for both of two conditions being true. This can be achieved by one or more "if" statements. Consider the following entrance condition for a course.

"Students must be aged 16 or over and have at least 4 GCSE passes."

This could be expressed

```
if age >= 16 then
    if passes >= 4 then
        accept onto course
    else
        reject application
    endif
else
    reject application
endif
```

This is rather cumbersome and is prone to error. A more satisfactory method is:

```
if age >= 16 AND passes >=4 then
    accept onto course
else
    reject application
endif
```

In this case the two conditions have been joined by the logical operator "AND". Both the expressions on either side of the "AND" have to be true for the whole expression to be true. If either of them are false the whole expression is false.

Most high level languages also provide an "OR" operator. In this case if either of the expressions is true the whole expression is true.

A "NOT" operator is also available to invert the truth of any Boolean expression.

The logical operators have priority of precedence over the conditional operators. This means that to get the usual meaning of the expression if age >= 16 and passes >= 4 The two conditional expressions are put in parentheses (brackets) thus

If (age >= 16 ) and ( passes >= 4) then ...

The "AND" and "OR" operators may be combined, e.g.

if ((height > 6 ) and (sex = male ))

or (( height > 5.5) and ( sex = female)) then ...

Pascal uses the keywords AND, OR and NOT

for the logical operators, C uses the symbols &&, || and ! this is shown in Fig. 7.5.

# ITERATION ... LOOPS

In Chapter 2 we saw that top down design uses three basic building blocks: sequence, selection and iteration. We have seen how to implement sequence and selection in C and Pascal so we now turn to iteration.

Most computer solutions to practical problems make extensive use of iteration. As we saw from the primitives in Chapter 2, computers can only perform very simple operations, but they do this very fast. So if a simple operation, or sequence of operations, is performed many hundreds (or even thousands) of times the effect is still a high speed performance. The solution to many complex calculations can be found by employing algorithms involving iteration to carry out a series of relatively simple steps repetitively. Iteration is a very powerful tool in the software designers armoury.

All program looping constructs have three elements;

- The initial state
- The loop body
- The continuation condition.

Program iterations consist of repeating a section of code a certain number of times. The programmers main concern when designing program loops is controlling the number of iterations. Programmers use the three elements above to achieve this.

A programmer sets the initial state by defining the value that various variables take immediately before entry into the loop body. This is only done once regardless of how many times the loop itself is executed.

| Operator | C | Pascal |
|---|---|---|
| and | && | AND |
| or | \|\| | OR |
| not | ! | NOT |

**Figure 7.5** Boolean operators in C and Pascal.

The loop body is the section of code that is repeated for each iteration of the loop. The continuation condition determines under what conditions the program leaves the loop and continues with the next statement.

Program loop structures can be classified in two different ways:

- **fixed** and **non-fixed**
- **pre-condition** and **post-condition**.

Fixed loops are easier to visualize than non-fixed. A fixed loop is when a certain section of code is required to be repeated a fixed number of times. It could possibly be 10 times or 20 or 25 times. Each time the program is run it always repeats the section of code the same number of times. Therefore the number of iterations is fixed. In this case the initial state involves setting a counter to an initial value, possibly 0 or 1. The loop body is the section of code. The continuation condition consists of adding one to the counter and checking to see if it has reached the final value. If it hasn't, the loop body is repeated, if it has the loop exits. A simple fixed loop is illustrated in Fig 7.6 using a flowchart.

The fixed loop is represented in many languages by the keyword "For". The keyword is used together with a starting value and an end value. It can be thought of as representing:

"for each value between the start value and the end value perform the loop body".

A loop control variable is normally used to "keep count" of the iterations.

Examples of "for" loops in C and Pascal are shown in Figs 7.7 and 7.8.

The general form of the Pascal "FOR" statement is:

FOR <variable> := <start_expression> TO <end_expression> DO <statement>;

The action of the FOR statement is to DO <statement> for each value of <variable> from <start_expression> to <end_expression>. First <variable> is assigned the value of <start_expression>. If <variable> is more than the value of <end_expression> then the whole statement terminates, otherwise the

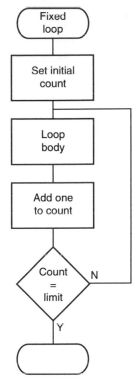

**Figure 7.6** A fixed loop structure.

<statement> is executed once. After the <statement> has been executed the value of <variable> is increased to the next ordinal value. (For integers this is an increment of one.) The value of <variable> is again compared with <end_expression> and if it is not greater, then the statement is repeated again, and so on.

Thus the value of the control variable counts from the value of the start expression to the value of the end expression. The value of the control variable may be used within the statement or it can be used simply to control the number of iterations.

The general form of the C "for" statement is:

for (expression 1; expression 2; expression 3) statement;

The action of the for statement is to:

1. evaluate expression 1
2. evaluate expression 2

```
for (count=1; count < 11; count++)
   printf("%d squared is %d",count,count*count);
scanf("%d %d",&start,&finish);
for (i = start; i <= finish; i++)
   sum = sum + i;
printf("%d is the sum of the numbers from %d to %d",sum,start,finish);
```

**Figure 7.7** Examples of for loops in C.

```
FOR count := 1 TO 10 DO
   WRITELN(count,' squared is ',count*count);

READLN(start,finish);
FOR i := start TO finish DO
   sum := sum + i;
WRITELN(sum,' is the sum of the numbers from ',start,'to',finish);
```

**Figure 7.8** Examples of FOR loops in Pascal.

3. if expression 2 is true then the statement is executed, otherwise the "for" statement terminates
4. expression 3 is evaluated
5. return to step 2.

The presence of any of expression 1, expression 2 and expression 3 is optional. This very flexible and powerful form of the for statement is most often used with expression 1 as assigning a start value, expression 2 as a test for the end value , and expression 3 as the control increment. A for statement simply used to control the number of iterations usually has a form similar to:

```
for ( i = 1; i < 10; i++) .......;
```

## Non-fixed loops

A non-fixed loop is where a section of code is repeated not a certain number of times, but until some condition is met. Non-fixed loops do not necessarily require a loop control variable of any kind. They are used where some event within the loop body controls whether another iteration is required. For example a program which reads a stream of input data until a terminating item is read. This could not be coded using a fixed loop, as the number of iterations depends on the input data. We saw in Chapter 2 that we could draw two different modular flowcharts to represent iteration (Fig. 2.22). The difference between them lies in the relative order of the loop body and the test for the continuation condition. With a pre-conditional loop the test occurs **before** the loop body, with a post-conditional loop the test occurs **after** the loop body.

The choice between the two different structures can be based on the answers to two questions.

■ Is a loop of zero iterations a valid situation?
■ Can the continuation condition be known before the loop body has executed once?

If the answer to the first question is yes, then a pre-condition loop is the most suitable. The body of a post-condition loop is executed **before** the continuation test, therefore the loop body will always be executed at least once. The body of a pre-condition loop is executed **after** the continuation test, therefore if the test is false the body is not executed at all, i.e. zero iterations.

If the answer to the second question is no, then a post-condition loop must be used. If the continuation condition is the result of some action within the loop body, then it cannot be known before the body has executed. With a post-condition loop the conditional test occurs **after** the body and so the condition is known.

## Programming of non-fixed loops

Both C and Pascal use the same keyword "while" for pre-condition loops. For post-condition loops both languages use a pair of keywords. Pascal uses REPEAT and UNTIL, C uses do and while. The format of the while loops in C and Pascal are similar:

> C:      while ( condition ) statement;

> Pascal: WHILE condition DO statement;

In both cases the statement continues to be executed while the condition is true. Note that if the statement does not affect the conditional test then the loop is never ending! The format of the post-condition loops in the two languages differ slightly;

> C:      do statement while ( condition);

> Pascal: REPEAT
>                 .
>                 .        Block of
>                 .        statements
>                 .
>          UNTIL condition;

The do–while loop in C executes the statement while the condition is true. The Pascal REPEAT–UNTIL structure creates an implicit block. The whole block (which could be a single statement) is repeated until the condition becomes true, that is while the condition is false. Figures 7.9–7.12 show pre- and post-conditional loops in C and Pascal.

## Loops as blocks

In all the loop structures, except for Pascal's REPEAT–UNTIL loop, the loop body consists of a single statement. Often a design calls for an iteration of several actions that cannot be coded into a single statement. In these cases the loop body is coded as a compound

```
REPEAT
  READLN(number);
  IF number MOD 2 = 0 THEN WRITELN("The number was even")
    ELSE WRITELN("The number was odd");
UNTIL number = 0;
```

**Figure 7.9** A post-conditional loop in Pascal.

```
do {
  scanf("%d",&number);
  if (0 == number % 2 )
    printf("The number was even");
  else printf("The number was odd");
  } while (number != 0);
```

**Figure 7.10** A post-conditional loop in C.

```
READLN(number);
WHILE number <> 0 DO
BEGIN
        IF number MOD 2 = 0 THEN WRITELN('The number was even')
                ELSE WRITELN('The number was odd');
        READLN(number);
END;
```

**Figure 7.11** A pre-conditional loop in Pascal.

```
scanf("%d", &number);
while( number != 0) {
        if (0 == number % 2 )
                printf('The number was even');
        else printf('The number was odd');
        scanf("%d", &number);
        }
```

**Figure 7.12** A pre-conditional loop in C.

statement or block (see Chapter 4). An alternative approach is to put all of the statements which comprise the loop body into a separate module, the loop body then becomes a single function/procedure call.

## Loops within loops

The controlled statement within a loop body may be any statement, including another loop statement. This leads to the possibility of having a loop within a loop. In this situation the loops are said to be nested. To distinguish between them, the loops are referred to as an inner loop and an outer loop. The inner loop first repeats its loop body the appropriate number of times, the outer loop repeats the whole of the inner loop for its required number of times. For fixed loops the actual number of iterations of the innermost loop is the product of the outer loop and inner loop individual iterations. Figure 7.13 shows implementations using nested loops in C and Pascal of the structure chart design from Figure 7.14.

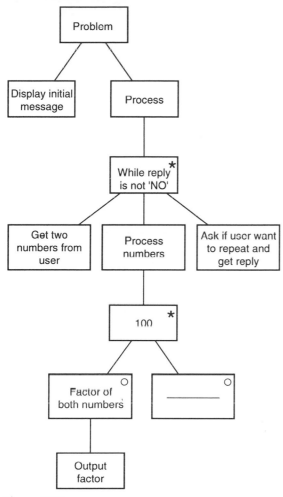

Figure 7.13.

## SUMMARY

❑ Selection is achieved using the "if" statement. Two forms are available to enable the programming of alternative actions.

❑ Conditional expressions are used which evaluate to "true" or "false".

❑ Loop constructs can be classified two different ways; fixed or non-fixed, and pre-condition or post-condition.

❑ All loop constructs have three elements; the initial state, the loop body and the continuation condition.

```
PROGRAM Factors(INPUT, OUTPUT);
  VAR number1,
    number2:INTEGER
    reply:CHAR;

PROCEDURE Message;
BEGIN
  WRITELN('Program to find common
  factors');
  WRITELN('Please input two
  integer numbers');
END

PROCEDURE Process_numbers;
VAR count : INTEGER;
BEGIN
  For count : = 1 TO 100 DO
    IF (count MOD number1 = 0)
    AND
    (count MOD number 2 = 0)
    THEN
    WRITELN(count,' is a factor
    of 'number1, 'and', number2);
END;

BEGIN
  Message;
  REPEAT
    READLN(number1,number2);
    Process_numbers;
    WRITELN('Another two numbers
(Y/N)');
    READLN(reply);
    UNTIL (reply = 'N') OR
(reply = 'n');
END.
```

```
#include < stdio.h >
int number1,
  number2;
char reply;
message()
{
  printf("Program to find common
  factors\n");
  printf("Please input two
  integer numbers\n");
}

process_numbers()
{
int count:
  for (count = 1; count < 100;
  count++)
    if ((count % number1
    ==0))&&
  (count % number2 == 0 ))
  printf("%d is a factor of %d
and %d\n",
count, number1,number2);
}
main()
{
  message();
  do {
  scanf("%d %d",&number1,&num
ber2);
  process_numbers();
  printf("Another two numbers
  (Y/N) :");
  reply = getchar();
  }while ((reply ! = 'N') &&
  (reply ! = 'n'));
  }
```

**Figure 7.14** Examples of nested loops.

# EXERCISES

1. Design and write a program which asks a user how old they are and if they have had their birthday this year. From the responses the program must calculate and display the year of the user's birth.

2. Design and write a program which reads two numbers and determines if the first one is exactly divisible by the second and display an appropriate message.

3. Design and write a program to find the real roots of a quadratic equation of the following form:

$$ax^2 + bx + c = 0.$$

   Given the formula, note that:

   (a) If $a = 0$ then the equation is linear $x = -c/b$

   (b) If $a = 0$ and $b = 0$ then the equation is void

   (c) If $b$ is less that $4ac$ there are no real roots.

4. Design and write a program to input whole numbers from the keyboard (with a suitable prompt), one at a time until a zero is entered. When input has terminated the program should display the sum of all the positive numbers entered and the number of negative numbers entered.

5. The number of words in a sentence, ending with a full stop, which is typed at the keyboard is required. Design and write a program to perform this task.

6. The population of a certain country grows by 1.5% per year.

   (a) Write a program which enables the user to input the current population, and which will display the population forecasts for the next five years.

   (b) Write a program to determine how many years it takes for the population to become one and a half times its current size.

7. A sequence of data consists of a series of positive numbers terminated by −1. Design and write a program to count how many times a number exceeds the previous number in the series, and how many times a number is less than its predecessor, e.g. the sequence

   4 2 9 9 3 7 7 7 3 3 2 −1

   should give

   less than predecessor    4
   more than predecessor   2

8. What will be displayed when either of the two program modules shown below are run.
   You may assume that all variables have been declared as integers.

```
exercise_8()
{
for ( i=1; i<12; i++) {
printf("%d times table\n",i);
for ( k=1; k<12; k++)
printf("%d x %d = %d\n",i,k,i*k);
printf("\n");
}
}
```

```
PROCEDURE Exercise_8;
BEGIN
  FOR i := 1 TO 12 DO
  BEGIN
  WRITELN(i,' times table');
  FOR k := 1 TO 12 DO
  WRITELN(i,' x ',k,' =
  ',i*k);
  WRITELN;
  END;
END;
```

9. Write two programs, one using a pre-condition loop, and one using a post-condition loop. The programs must read a series of characters ending with a full stop, and display the number of occurrences of the upper case letter "Q".

# Layout and style

## INTRODUCTION

The provision of documentation is one of the most neglected areas of software. Because the provision of the necessary documentation to support the program is not seen as an essential requirement, it is seldom done or done properly. Indeed it is almost invariably left until after the program has been developed, and is then seen as delaying the release of the program. It should be one of the fundamentals of software management that no program is allowed to be used until sufficient documentation has been produced.

A complete computer system could be described as consisting of hardware, software and documentation. Whereas no customer would knowingly accept faulty hardware or software, inadequate or poor documentation is tolerated.

## WHO IS THE DOCUMENTATION FOR?

There are three groups who need to refer to program documentation:

- Programmers
- Operators
- Users.

### Programmers

Once having been written, programs may used in their operating environment for periods of ten years or more. During this time they will be subject to many alterations and enhancements to reflect the changing needs of the users. This task is known as software maintenance, and may consume as much as 50% of the time spent in developing the program. This means that the average programmer spends half his or her time working with programs which were most likely written by other programmers, who may no longer be available to be consulted on the details of their code. Unless the programs were initially well written and adequately documented, maintenance programming can be time consuming and costly.

### Operators

In a situation in which programs are run by operators (e.g. on a large organization's mainframe computer) which involves possible interaction between the program and the system, or the program and other programs, at run time, it is essential that the operators are aware of the tasks carried out by the program.

### Users

The user is the person or section of an organization for whom a program is run. The users only interaction with a program is via its inputs and outputs.

The user must understand what input is required by the program, and the nature of the data output by the program. In an interactive environment, particularly with microcomputers, the role of user and operator are combined.

# DOCUMENTATION FOR PROGRAMMERS

The documentation required to enable a program to be maintained over its lifespan may be divided into two categories: internal and external.

## Internal documentation

This covers the aspects of programs which are embodied in the syntax of the programming language. It is concerned with the layout and style of the program listing. Some of the important points are:

- Meaningful names used for data items and program modules.
- Comments to clarify the function of the program as a whole and the modules comprising the program.
- Clarity of style and layout.
- Use of symbolic names for constants and literals.

This is covered in more detail in Chapter 9.

## External documentation

This category covers the supporting documentation which should be maintained in a manual or folder accompanying the program. It is essential that as changes are made to a program, its external documentation is updated at the same time.

Out of date documentation can be misleading to a maintenance programmer and result in time being wasted.

External documentation should include :

- A **current** listing of the source program plus any memory maps, cross-references, etc., that can be obtained from the assembly or compilation process.

- Instructions on how to produce an executable program from the source code. Details of the compiler, linker, etc., are required and any configuration details should be included. This may be in the form of a script or Makefile.
- The program specification that defines the purpose and mode of operation of the program.
- The program design, e.g. structure diagrams, flowcharts.
- An explanation of any formulae or complex calculations in the program. Some background information concerning the programs sphere of operation may also be useful.
- A specification of the data being processed:
  (a) Data accepted or displayed on the screen
  (b) Items in reports
  (c) External files processed (including record and field formats)
  (d) All data being described in terms of its size, format, type and structure.
- Where applicable, the format of screens used to interact with users and of printed reports.
- The test data used to validate the program.
- Any special directions of importance to programmers who may be involved in amending or enhancing the program. For example restrictions on size of data structures, etc.

# USER DOCUMENTATION

The user documentation should contain all the necessary information to enable someone to use the program without recourse to the programmer or other sources of information. When writing user documentation the background knowledge and computer familiarity of the intended user should be taken into account. A user may have detailed knowledge of a programs subject matter, but little computer experience.

Instructions on how to operate the program, e.g. commands or menu options must be given clearly and concisely. Often an example of a typical program session or run is helpful. Diagrams showing typical screen displays can be used to give a new user confidence.

Details of the format of the input data must be given. In general the program prompts should invite input of the correct format, but this may be supported with more detailed information in the documentation.

# PROGRAM STYLE AND LAYOUT

Most modern block structured languages are free format. The meaning of a program is not affected by how it is laid out on a page. In fact there are few rules concerning the layout of C or Pascal. The main ones being:

■ Any number of spaces may be placed between symbols.
■ No spaces may be placed within symbols
■ A new line can occur anywhere a space may occur (except within literal strings).

Note: symbols include identifiers, keywords, numbers, operators (+, :=, ==, \ +=), etc.

This freedom of layout can be used to improve the readability of programs. Neat and consistent layout is important to comprehension, and can be used to highlight the structure of the program.

The liberal use of blank lines, distinguishing case and indented paragraphing makes a program appear more elegant and easier to read.

Compare the program segments in Figs 8.1 or 8.2 (see page 74). They are functionally identical, the only difference is the layout.

It is possible to draw up some broad guidelines regarding layout.

■ Distinct parts of the program such as the header, variable declarations, and module body should be separated with blank lines.
■ Each block within the program is indented to clearly show the beginning and end.
■ If the language supports it reserved words are highlighted in upper case to differentiate them from programmer devised identifiers.

There are no accepted hard and fast rules governing layout. However, most organizations adopt what is referred to as a house standard. House standards are useful where many programmers are working on the same or associated projects. If all the program listings are laid out in the same manner then it becomes much easier for programmers to read and understand each others programs.

As an example of a house standard the following is the Pascal standard for Brunel College of Arts and Technology, Faculty of Engineering:

1. All program entities (constants, variables, procedures, etc.) should be given a name which reflects their use within the program.
2. Each statement should start on a new line. The only exception to this rule is where several variables are being assigned the same value, e.g.

   count := 0; limit := 0, nextvalue :- 0;

3. Statements which cannot be conveniently written on a single line should be carefully broken at a point which reflects the structure. Second and subsequent lines should be indented.
4. Each logical section of the program (e.g. procedure header, variable declarations, main block) should be preceded and followed by one or more blank lines.
5. Short comments may be placed on the same line as the code to which they refer. Longer comments should be on a separate line preceded and followed by one or more blank lines.
6. Reserved language words (e.g. IF, BEGIN, UNTIL, etc.) should be in upper case. Programmer devised names should be in lower case, though procedure names may start with a capital letter.
7. The reserved words BEGIN, END and REPEAT should always appear on a line by themselves. The reserved word UNTIL should always start a new line.
8. All the lines between a BEGIN–END pair and a REPEAT–UNTIL pair should be indented. The preferred indent is two or three spaces. Inner blocks should be further indented by the same amount.

```
procedure countelements;
{Given a sorted array this
procedure prints each element
and the number of occurrences of
that element}
var i,count:integer;begin
count:=1;for i:=1 to arraysize-1
do
if values[i]=values[i+1] then
count:=count+1 else
begin
write(values[i],count);count:=1;
end;write(values[arraysize]count
);
end;


PROCEDURE Countelements;

{ Given a sorted array this pro-
cedure prints each element and
the number of occurrences of
that element}

VAR i,
count : INTEGER;

BEGIN
  count := 1;
  FOR i := 1 TO arraysize -1 DO
  IF values[i] = values[i+1]
THEN
    count := count +1;
  ELSE
  BEGIN
    WRITE(values[i], count);
    count := 1;
  END;
  WRITE(values[arraysize],
count);
END;
```

**Figure 8.1** Examples of layout in Pascal.

```
countelements()
/*Given a sorted array this
function prints each element and
the number of occurrences of
that element*/ {int i,count;
count=1;for
(i=1;i!=arraysize;i++)
if
(values[i]==values[i+1])count=
count+1; else {printf("%d
%d",values[i],count);count=1;
}printf("%d %d",values[array-
size]count);
}

countelements()
/* Given a sorted array this
procedure prints each
element and the number of occur-
rences of that element */
{
int i,
  count;
count = 1;
for (i = 1; i != arraysize; i++)
  if (values[i] == values[i+1])
    count = count +1;
  else
  {
  printf("%d %d",values[i],
count);
  count = 1;
  }
printf("%d %d",values[array-
size], count); }
```

**Figure 8.2** Examples of layout in C.

Figure 8.3 contains a program which breaks the house rules.

Similar rules could be applied to programs written in C. There has been much discussion over the years concerning C brace style, that is where to position the opening and closing braces. The original Kernighan and Richie style is much like that adopted for Pascal programs. Later advocates of C programming have adopted various different styles. Check with your house standard to see which brace style you should adopt.

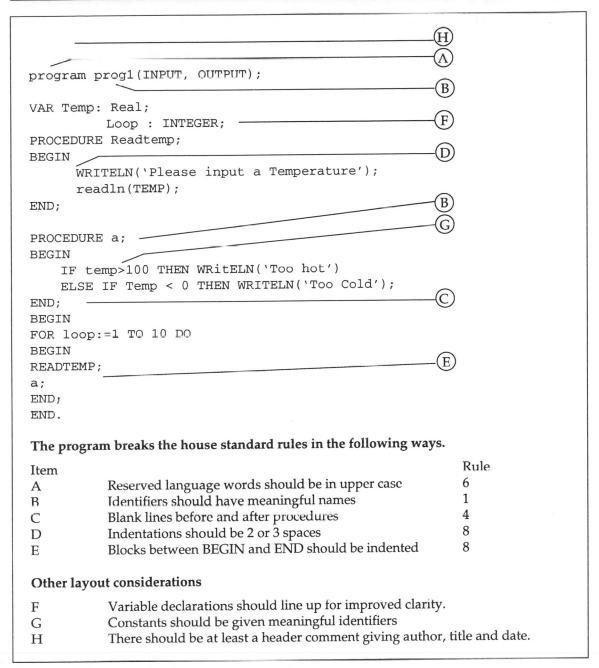

```
                                                                    (H)
                                                                    (A)
program prog1(INPUT, OUTPUT);
                                                                    (B)
VAR Temp: Real;
          Loop : INTEGER;                                           (F)
PROCEDURE Readtemp;
BEGIN                                                               (D)
      WRITELN('Please input a Temperature');
      readln(TEMP);
END;                                                                (B)
                                                                    (G)
PROCEDURE a;
BEGIN
    IF temp>100 THEN WRitELN('Too hot')
    ELSE IF Temp < 0 THEN WRITELN('Too Cold');
END;                                                                (C)
BEGIN
FOR loop:=1 TO 10 DO
BEGIN
READTEMP;                                                           (E)
a;
END;
END.
```

**The program breaks the house standard rules in the following ways.**

| Item | | Rule |
|------|-------------------------------------------------------|------|
| A | Reserved language words should be in upper case | 6 |
| B | Identifiers should have meaningful names | 1 |
| C | Blank lines before and after procedures | 4 |
| D | Indentations should be 2 or 3 spaces | 8 |
| E | Blocks between BEGIN and END should be indented | 8 |

**Other layout considerations**

| | |
|---|---|
| F | Variable declarations should line up for improved clarity. |
| G | Constants should be given meaningful identifiers |
| H | There should be at least a header comment giving author, title and date. |

**Figure 8.3** This program breaks the house rules as shown.

## USE OF COMMENTS

We saw in Chapter 4 how to put comments into a high level language source text, but have not considered what information the comments should contain. The ease of maintenance of a program depends to large extent on how well the program has been commented. The amount of information, the positioning and layout of the comments all contribute to the understanding of a program.

A fully commented program should contain at least:

- A main header comment at the top of the listing giving the program name, the authors name, the date and version number of the program.
- A descriptive comment giving a brief explanation of the programs function.
- Comments relating to each variable declaration stating the purpose of the variables.
- A header comment for each module (procedure/function) in the program. This should state the modules functions and its input and output data.

There may also be comments referring to sections of code that are particularly significant to the program's operation, or are particularly complex.

The main and module header comments should be laid out in such a way that they stand out from the rest of the program. A common practice is to surround them with a box made up of distinguishing characters. A suitable layout is shown in Fig. 8.4.

The information contained in a comment should add understanding to a program not simply repeat the language statement. The comment in the line:

```
scanf("%d", temperature); /* read
in the temperature */
```

tells us very little extra than can be deduced from the program. Comments can used to explain **why** the program needs to perform a particular action, **what** is performed should be obvious from the listing.

## SUMMARY

❑ Documentation is an important part of software production.

❑ Different types of documentation are required for different categories of user.

❑ Programs should be laid out to an agreed house standard.

❑ Comments should be clear and add understanding to a program.

```
      /*************************************************
      *                                               *
      *      Program name: Comment Example            *
      *      Author name: A. Programmer               *
      *      Date: 1/1/94                             *
      *      Version:2.5                              *
      *                                               *
      *************************************************/
```

**Figure 8.4** A header comment.

# EXERCISES

1. Layout one of the following sections of code according to your agreed house standard. You may assume the code is correct and does not need to be changed.

```
PROGRAM Rainfall(input,OUTPUT);{calculate the rainfall over
several days}VAR AVERAGE, ToTalrain,inches:REAL;
numberofdays,counter: integer;
{ First read the number of days, then the rainfall for each day.
Output the average rainfall over the period}
begin READLN(numberOfDays);{get howmany days}
TOTALRAIN:=0;Counter:=1; WHILE counter <= NumberOfDays
DO BEGIN
READLN(inches); totalrain:=totalrain+inches;{add to the total}
counter:=counter+1;END;
IF totalrain =
0.0 THEN WRITELN('There was no rain')
ELSE
BEGIN
  Average:= totalrain/numberofdays;
  writeln('The average rainfall was',AVERAGE:7:3);
  END;
END.

main()/*calculate the rainfall over
several days*/{ float AVERAGE, ToTalrain,inches;
int numberofdays,counter: integer;
/* First read the number of days, then the rainfall for each day.
Output the average rainfall over the period*/
{scanf("%d", numberofdays);/*get howmany days*/
ToTalrain=0;counter=1; while (counter <= numberofdays
){
scanf("%f", inches);
ToTalrain:=ToTalrain+inches;/*add to the total*/
counter:=counter+1;} IF (totalrain == 0.0) printf("There was no
rain\n"); else{
  AVERAGE = ToTalrain/numberofdays;
  printf("The average rainfall was %7.3f\n",AVERAGE);
  }
}
```

2. How can software maintenance be made easier by good documentation?
3. Why are comments important in programs?

# 9 Testing

## INTRODUCTION

Just as any other engineering product has to be tested, so we must test software. Simply running the program to see if it works isn't good enough. We must test it in a clearly defined, rigorous manner. It is equally, if not more important, to test the response of the software to unusual or abnormal inputs as it is to normal inputs. To enable testing to be carried out in a clearly defined manner test documentation should be produced. This documentation is produced at the design stage, i.e. **before** any coding is done.

The minimum test documentation consists of the test specification (also called a test plan) and the test log. The test specification is a description of what is to be tested and how. The test log is a record of the results obtained from carrying out the tests.

## THE TEST SPECIFICATION

When writing the test specification it is necessary to refer to the original program specification to see how the system is expected to perform under various conditions. A vague or imprecise program specification leads to ambiguous test results.

### Format of a test specification

1. *Identity of the program to be tested*. This will be the name of the program and may also include a version number and date. Any other data needed to identify the program should be included here.

2. *Test methods*. This should describe the approach to the test, e.g. is it to be off-line/on-line, real-time, single step, connected to external equipment, etc. If the testing involves the setting up of some initial conditions an explanation of how this is to done should be included.

3. *Test data*. If the testing requires some data to be set up in advance, e.g. a file of input information, this should be detailed. The data used for testing normal and abnormal testing should be clearly defined.

4. *The tests*. These should define the combination of inputs needed to test the system and the expected outputs. Tests may be independent or in related groups. Each test should state its purpose and be numbered. Each input to the program should tested for all possible states which may occur, both normal and abnormal. If there is a very large number of states, e.g. numerical input, a sample across the range should be chosen. For more complex tests decision tables or flowcharts may be necessary to define the sequence of inputs and the expected outputs.

## THE TEST LOG

This should be a list of the tests in the test specification. Each test is identified by its number. The actual output obtained from the program is noted. By comparing this actual input with the expected outputs a pass/fail indication can be given for each test. If there is a large number of tests, a summary of the passes and fails at the end can be useful.

## CHOOSING TEST DATA VALUES

The most critical element in the production of a good test specification is the selection of the test data values. Simply choosing some typical values at random will not effectively test the software. Experience has shown that there a several categories of data which are best at revealing possible errors.

- Boundary values
- Special values
- Typical values
- Abnormal values.

### Boundary values

Testing with boundary values aims to test those parts of the program concerned with conditional operations, i.e. loop conditions and selection operations. Tests are devised which involve data values just below, at and just above the boundary value. Normally these values can be deduced from the program specification.

For example, if a program is required to process whole numbers up to twenty in a particular way and numbers over twenty in a different manner, then suitable test data values for this boundary would be 19, 20 and 21.

### Special values

A special value is any data value which is to be treated by the software as different from all other values. There are some values which should be treated as special for all programs.

*Zero*. Although zero is mathematically just a number it does have some unique characteristics. Adding and subtracting it has no effect, multiplying by it always gives zero as a result, and dividing by it will normally produce an error. Because of this, the value zero should always be included in a set of test data for numerical inputs.

*Null data*. A null input is where no data is input (**note**: no data is **not** the same as zero input!). Inputting of no data is often not an option where numerical values are concerned. With character strings, however, the program's response to a null or zero length string should always be tested.

Other special values will depend on the program specification. Any value which is specifically mentioned must be treated as special and should be tested explicitly.

### Typical values

Here a range of values representing typical normal data is chosen. The range should include all the various categories which the program is expected to handle. If the data is numeric for example then tests should be devised to cover small numbers, large numbers, negative numbers, whole numbers, numbers with decimal parts, etc. If the data is character based then tests using upper case, lower case, non-alphanumeric, etc., data should be devised.

### Abnormal values

Abnormal inputs include any data which is not in the set of acceptable input data. This may be values of a different type, e.g. character data for a numeric input or a decimal number for an integer input. Abnormal values also include data which are of the same type as the expected input but out of the allowed range. For example a program which required a person's age could reasonably be expected to reject inputs of −3 and 547. It is important to test a program's response to abnormal data. Users are well known for typing exactly what the program designer didn't expect. Any program that is designed for serious use should not crash or misbehave simply because of user input.

For some programs the order in which the tests are carried out may affect the results. It is possible for some error conditions not to affect the current test, but to change the programs behaviour to future inputs. These errors are very hard to find. Repeating a set of tests in a different order can sometimes help to uncover these elusive bugs.

# A TYPICAL TEST SPECIFICATION

Suppose a program has been written to the following specification.

A program is required to input a daily pay rate and calculate the gross annual salary (365 × Daily Pay) and tax as follows:
  (a) No tax payable on the first £3500
  (b) 25% tax rate over £3500 and up to £20,000
  (c) 33% tax rate over £20,000.
The program should display the gross salary, the tax payable and the net salary. All output shown to two decimal places.

We must study the specification to determine the tests we will apply to any program written to this specification. We need to produce test data for each of the four cases listed above, i.e. boundary, special, typical and abnormal data.

First we must identify the inputs to the program. In this case there is only one, namely the daily pay rate. It is reasonable to assume that the daily rate will not be a whole number. Work rates normally include pounds and pence not just whole numbers of pounds.

Also quite clearly the daily pay rate should not be zero or a negative value. Setting an upper limit is more difficult, as the specification does not call for one we will assume there is no limit.

To choose the boundary values we need to look more closely at the program specification. There are clearly boundaries at gross annual pay of £3500 and £20,000. These can be worked backwards to give boundaries for the input daily pay of £9.59 and £54.79.

The only special value we need to consider is zero.

Typical values should be chosen to give at least two tests in each of the three bands, £0–3500, £3500–£20,000, above £20,000. Also test data involving whole numbers and decimal numbers must be included.

The test data for abnormal inputs falls into two categories: abnormal numeric data and non-numeric data. As we saw above the only two cases of abnormal numeric data are zero and negative numbers. Non-numeric abnormal test data may include any alphabetic or punctuation characters.

## The test specification

*Program under test.* A tax calculation program, 'TAXCALC' written on 28/3/94 by A. N. Other.

*Test methods.* The tests are to be carried out on-line. For each test the program is run by typing its name at the keyboard and pressing <ENTER>. There are no special setup requirements.

*The tests.* The tests to be carried out and their associated data are given in Fig. 9.1.

The test log will record the actual output generated by the program for each test. By comparing with the expected outcome each test can be given a pass or fail indication.

It is important to realize that even if a program passes all the tests in the test specification there may still be errors in it. Apart from very trivial programs, we can never be certain that we have found all the errors in a piece of software. We can only say that the software passes all the tests we have devised for it. Hopefully, if the tests have been designed with care, the software will have few, if any, errors. But we can never be sure that a piece of software is flawless.

**Figure 9.1**

| Test | Purpose | Input data | | | Expected output |
|------|---------|------------|------|------|-----------------|
| *Tests for normal data* | | | | | |
| | | gross | tax | net | |
| 1a | No tax under £3500 | 5 | 1825.00 | 0.00 | 1825.00 |
| 1b | Decimal value accepted | 6.54 | 2387.10 | 0.00 | 2387.10 |
| 2a | 25% tax band | 10 | 3650.00 | 37.50 | 3612.50 |
| 2b | 25% tax band | 38.95 | 14,216.75 | 2679.19 | 11,537.56 |
| 3a | 33% tax band | 60.56 | 22,104.40 | 4651.10 | 17,453.30 |
| 3b | 33% tax band | 112.56 | 41,084.40 | 9396.10 | 31,688.30 |
| 4a | 25% boundary | 9.52 | 3493.05 | 0.00 | 3493.05 |
| 4b | 25% boundary | 9.59 | 3500.35 | 0.09 | 3500.26 |
| 4c | 25% boundary | 9.61 | 3507.65 | 1.91 | 3505.74 |
| 5a | 33% boundary | 54.7 | 19,965.50 | 4116.38 | 15849.13 |
| 5b | 33% boundary | 54.79 | 19,998.35 | 4124.59 | 15,873.76 |
| 5c | 33% boundary | 54.83 | 20,012.95 | 4128.24 | 15,884.71 |
| *Test for abnormal data* | | | | | |
| 6 | zero daily pay | 0 | | | Zero or error message |
| 7 | Negative daily pay | −10.5 | | | Error message |
| 8a | Non-numeric data | A | | | Error message |
| 8b | Non-numeric data | 3.G | | | Error message |
| 8c | Non-numeric data | 12Z4 | | | Error message |
| 8d | Non-numeric data | * | | | Error message |
| 9 | Null data | <ENTER> | | | Error message or an invitation to re-enter the data. |

# FINDING ERRORS

A program that fails any of the tests in the test specification is flawed and must be corrected. We saw in Chapter 3 that a program may have errors of syntax, these are detected by the compiler. The errors detected during testing are errors of logic. These logical errors can occur for one of two reasons:

■ Errors in design, i.e. the chosen design does not produce a solution to the problem.
■ Errors in implementation, i.e. the design is correct but errors are introduced when the design is implemented as a program.

A program which has logical errors will compile and run, but does not produce the expected results. Logical errors are much more difficult to find than syntax errors. The compiler is of no help, the program is syntactically correct.

In order to find logical errors it is necessary to examine the way in which the program behaves. Usually the problem can be narrowed down to a specific area of the program. If the program produces the correct results for the majority inputs, and only fails for a certain type of input, or under certain conditions, then the error is most likely in that part of the program which deals with the inputs causing the failure.

Having narrowed down the problem it is sometimes useful to conduct more tests. These extra tests are designed to exercise the suspect part of the problem. The results of these tests may give more information to enable the actual error to be identified.

Other techniques which can be used to identify errors include:

- Trace tables and dry running
- Displaying intermediate results.
- Testing individual modules separately
- Single stepping through the program.

The technique known as dry running can be used to find errors in a design or an implementation. The essence of the technique is for the person carrying out the test to effectively become the computer. If it is the design that is being tested then the tester performs each of the actions, selections, etc., specified in the structure diagram, flowchart or pseudocode. A dry run can also be done on the implementation, or program, derived from a design. In this case the tester reads each program statement and executes it according to the rules of the language. Dry runs are most effective when combined with a trace table. When drawing up a trace table the first task is to identify all the variables and conditions used in the program. These form the column headings for the table. When the dry run is performed each step or statement is represented by one line in the trace table. The values for any variables that have been changed are entered into the table. The last entry in any column is taken as the current value of that variable. The dry run works through the program step by step filling in the table. In input data is required then this is read from the test specification. In this way the detailed actions taken by the program are examined and any errors located. Figure 9.2 gives an example of a trace table.

A simple but effective way of tracking down problems is to add extra lines to the program to display the values of critical variables at certain points. When using this technique care must be taken to ensure that the extra lines added do not themselves alter the behaviour of the program.

Individual modules (procedures/functions) can be tested separately, this will normally entail writing extra software. The extra software, variously known as a test harness or test driver, is used to provide data to the module under test and receive back results from it. In this way the module can be tested in isolation. The danger with this method lies with the problem of testing the test driver. If the test driver is simply some input and output statements then there should be little problem. But care should be taken to ensure the test driver does not become as complex as the module under test.

Tools known as debuggers are available to aid in the search for program errors. These tools enable the user to take control of the execution of the program. The facilities provided usually include: single stepping through each line/statement of the program separately; monitoring, or watching, program variables; ability to change the value of variables during a program run, etc. Debug tools are very useful in detecting errors in complex programs. However for simple programs they are rarely necessary. Reliance on debug tools robs the programmer of the clearer insight into a program's working that other methods give.

## SOURCES OF ERRORS

There are many causes of logical errors in programs, but several occur frequently enough to be a good place to start looking. some of the most common causes of error are:

- Wrongly initialized variables
- Bad block structuring
- Confusion of variable names
- Misplaced punctuation
- Typing errors
- Bad conditional expressions.

### Wrongly initialized variables

It should not be assumed that on entry into the program, or module, that a variable has

| line number | number1 | number2 | count | count% number1 | count% number2 |
|---|---|---|---|---|---|
| 4 | 2 | 3 | 5 | | |
| 5 | 2 | 3 | 5 | 1 | 2 |
| 4 | 2 | 3 | 6 | | |
| 5 | 2 | 3 | 6 | 0 | 0 |
| 6 | 2 | 3 | 6 | | |
| 4 | 2 | 3 | 7 | | |
| 5 | 2 | 3 | 7 | 1 | 1 |
| 4 | 2 | 3 | 8 | | |
| 5 | 2 | 3 | 8 | 0 | 2 |
| 4 | 2 | 3 | 9 | | |
| 5 | 2 | 39 | 1 | 0 | |
| 4 | 2 | 3 | 10 | | |
| 5 | 2 | 3 | 10 | 0 | 1 |
| 4 | 2 | 3 | 11 | | |
| 5 | 2 | 3 | 11 | 1 | 2 |
| 4 | 2 | 3 | 12 | | |
| 5 | 2 | 3 | 12 | 0 | 0 |
| 6 | 2 | 3 | 12 | | |

Line No.

```
1 process numbers( )
2 {
3 int count;
4 for (count = 1; count <
    100; count++)
5 if ((count % number 1 ==
    0 ) &&
    (count % number2 == 0))
6 printf("%d is a factor of %d
    and %d\n",count,
    number1, number2);
7 }
```

**Figure 9.2** Part of a trace table for the program segment shown.

any specific value. Unless the variable has been assigned a value it should not be used on the right-hand side of an expression or as a parameter. For example the expression

```
count = count + 1;
```

is commonly used to count the number of occurrences of a particular action. It relies for its success on "count" being zero before the first occurrence. This cannot be guaranteed.

Some compilers initialize global variables to zero, some do not. Variables local to a module can never be guaranteed to have any particular value on entry to the module. All variables should be initialized before use.

## Bad block structuring

An error commonly made by novice programmers is forgetting to make groups of statements into blocks or compound statements. This is particularly so after conditional, if statements. For example:

```
IF temperature > max_temp THEN
    WRITELN(' Heater turned
    off');
    heater := off;
```

should be:

```
IF temperature > max_temp THEN
    BEGIN
    WRITELN(' Heater turned
    off');
    heater := off;
    END;
```

A similar situation occurs with loop constructs, e.g.

```
while ( i < 10 )
    printf("%d squared is %d\n",i,
    i*i);
    i++;
```

is incorrect as the value of "'i'" is unchanged within the loop. The correct construct is:

```
while ( i < 10 )
    {
    printf("%d squared is %d\n",i,
    i*i);
    i++;
    }
```

## Confusion of variable names

When choosing names for variables care should be taken to ensure each name is distinct from the others. A common source of error is where the programmer types one name instead of a similar one. If the two variables are of the same data type then the compiler will accept the wrong name. This error can sometimes be very difficult to spot. When reading the program listing it is human nature to read what we expect to see, not necessarily what is actually there. If possible avoid names that differ in only one letter or number. Variable names like value1, value2, value3, etc., are easily confused and not very meaningful.

## Misplaced punctuation

In most cases putting a semicolon or bracket in the wrong place will cause a syntax error. There are a few occasions however when an incorrectly placed semicolon will cause the semantics (i.e. meaning) of a statement to change whilst remaining syntactically correct. Consider the following segments of Pascal:

*Correct*:

```
IF a = b THEN
    c := d;
```

*Incorrect*:

```
IF a = b THEN;
    c := d;
```

There is a strong tendency amongst novice programmers to put a semicolon on the end of each line, rather than at the end of each statement. In the example above, the incorrect version will assign "d" to "c" regardless of whether "a" is equal to "b" or not. The semicolon after the THEN terminates the IF statement, so what is executed if "a" does equal "b" is a null statement. A similar problem can occur with for statements.

*Correct*:

```
for (i=0; i<10; i++)
    printf("%d squared is
    %d\n",i,i*i);
```

*Incorrect*:

```
for (i=0; i<10; i++);
    printf("%d squared is
    %d\n",i,i*i);
```

The correct statement will give ten lines of output, one for each value of i from 0 to 9. The incorrect version will only give one line of output.

Misplaced or missing brackets can also cause logical errors. If the open and close brackets are unmatched the compiler will indicate a syntax error. If they are matched but in the wrong place then usually the program will compile successfully.

## Typing errors

Simple typographical errors, such as spelling mistakes, usually cause syntax errors. There are occasions when a simple one character exchange does not cause a syntax error. A common error of this type is where a plus (+) is replaced with a minus (–) sign or vice versa. This will clearly have an adverse effect upon the calculation, but does not usually cause a syntax error.

## Bad conditional expressions

A wrong choice of expression in a conditional statement can introduce subtle errors into a program. Sometimes the difference between, for example, "less than" and "not greater than" is not appreciated by the programmer leading to erroneous behaviour by the program. The condition associated with a loop construct must be chosen with care. It is possible to have a terminating condition which, under some circumstances, can never be true. Consider the following program segment:

```
scanf("%d", number);
do {
   printf("%d squared is %d",
   number,number*number);
   number = number + 5;
   } while ( number != 100 );
```

This would at first sight appear to display the squares of numbers from some starting value up to 100. But if the user enters a value above 100 then the condition in the "while" statement will always be true. Also if the user enters a number below 100 which is not an exact multiple of 5, then "number" will take values less than 100 and more than 100 but never exactly 100.

Floating point numbers should in general never be tested for equality. Due to rounding errors two numbers may be equal to several places of decimals, and therefore for most practical purposes can be considered equal, but if the numbers differ in the seventh or eighth decimal place then an equality test will fail. It is better to test if the absolute value of the difference between the two numbers is less than a small amount.

Combining conditional expressions using logical operators can cause errors. Particular care should be taken when negative conditions are used. One common mistake is code similar to:

```
REPEAT
   .
   .
   .
   READLN(reply);
UNTIL ( reply <> 'Y') OR ( reply
<> 'y' );
```

Careful study of the UNTIL condition will show that, regardless of the value of "reply", the condition will always be true. Changing the OR to an AND will correct the problem, or using a positive condition, e.g.

```
UNTIL ( reply = 'n' ) OR ( reply =
'N');
```

## SUMMARY

❑ Testing should be undertaken in a rigorous and controlled manner.

❑ All tests should be clearly documented.

❑ Test data must be chosen with care, not randomly.

❑ Finding logical errors can be a very time consuming process.

❑ Logical errors are often caused by simple typing mistakes.

# EXERCISES

1. A program has been written to meet the following specification:

   To check an applicant's level of insurance no-claim discount.

   Inputs:

   Years since last claim

   Applicant's age

   Outputs:

   Level of discount as a percentage.

   If the applicant has not claimed for 6 years – 40%

   If the applicant has not claimed for 4 years – 30%

   If the applicant is under 25 years of age the discount is reduced by 10%.

   Explain how you would undertake the testing of the program.

   Include in your answer a sample of part of the test specification. **Do not write the program.**

2. Dry run your solution to Exercise 7.7. Produce a trace table using the following data as the input.

   34  56  3  56  18  109  200  14  8  62  −1

3. Find four errors in one of the following sections of code. For each error state whether it is a syntax or logical error.

```
PROCEDURE Test;
  size = 1;
  REPEAT
    area := size * size;
    size := size + 2;
    WRITELN(area)
  UNTIL area = 20;
END;


Test();
{
size = 1;
do
  area = size * size;
  size = size + 2;
  printf("%d",area)
while (area = 20);
}
```

# 10 Accessing files

## INTRODUCTION

So far all the programs we have met have used the keyboard as the source of all data, and the VDU screen as the destination of all output.

Sometimes it is convenient to prepare input data in advance of running a program, particularly if the amount of data is large. Equally, there may be occasions when program output needs to be retained for future processing. Under these circumstances the backing store of the computer can be used to store the data. Most computer operating systems manage the backing store as a system of files.

## FILE FORMATS

The way that data are stored in a file determines how they can be accessed and processed. The simplest method of storing data in a file is sequentially, where data items follow each other. Each item of data is stored after the last item. That is, they are stored in the same order as they written to the file. The file can be imagined as a long paper tape, with each item written on to the tape in turn. The structure of a sequential file is shown in Fig. 10.1.

The disadvantage of sequential files is the speed of access. If an item towards the end of the file is required then all the data before the required item must be read first. To overcome this, and other problems, random access files are used. The programming for random

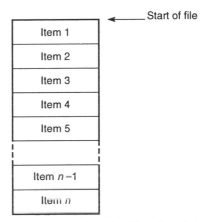

**Figure 10.1** A sequential file of length $n$ data items.

access files is beyond the scope of this book, we shall restrict ourselves to sequential files.

### Text and binary files

The information in a file can be coded in one of two ways: binary and text. For binary files the information is stored in the same format as it is held in the main memory of the computer. The information in text files is stored in the same format as that displayed to a screen, usually as ASCII characters.

If the information is held in a text file then each item of data is of variable length. The data items can be delimited by a space, a comma or a newline. For information held in binary format, each item takes up a predetermined amount of space. The actual space used depends on the data type, for example:

| Integer | 2 bytes |
| Real | 7 bytes |
| Character | 1 byte. |

There are advantages and disadvantages to each method. Text files may be read and created using a standard text editor. They may be printed onto a hard copy for storage or study. Being in human readable form no special facilities are required to read text files. Text files are very convenient for transferring data between dissimilar programs. As the ASCII code is an internationally recognized standard most packages will work successfully with text files.

The main disadvantage with text files is the speed of processing. Because the data has to be converted from ASCII to binary, or vice versa, when a file is read, or written, text files tend to be slower than binary files. There is also a potential problem when reading text files with numeric data. If the file has been created using a text editor there is the possibility of a non-numeric character due to a typing error. Therefore the data not only has to be converted, but also has to be checked for consistency.

The disadvantage with binary files is that they are not in human readable form. A special program usually has to be written to display the contents in a meaningful way. However access is much faster. With binary files it is usually more difficult to mix different data types in one file. As each data item is of different length, knowing where one item finishes and the next one starts can be a problem.

# PROGRAMS FOR FILE ACCESS

From the programming point of view accessing data in files is a four stage process:

1. Declare a file variable
2. Associate the file variable with an actual file
3. 'Open' the file
4. Read or write data from or to the file.

## File variables

All reference to a data file from within a program is made via the file variable, or file descriptor. This is usually a variable with a special data type, but may sometimes be a simple integer. The file variable is declared using the usual language syntax.

For a C program this is of the form:

```
FILE *data_file;
```

"FILE" is a special data type (see structures in Chapter 11), it is usually defined in "stdio.h", so this must be included in the program. The asterisk denotes a pointer type. The variable name, in this case "data_file" can be any legal identifier.

For a Pascal program this is of the form:

```
VAR data_file : FILE OF < data
type >;
```
or
```
VAR data_file : TEXT;
```

The first form is for binary files, the second form for text files. For binary files the <data type> is the datatype of the data to be stored in the file, e.g. REAL, INTEGER, etc.

## Associating the actual file name

The mechanism for associating an actual file name with the file variable is, to a certain extent, system dependent. Different operating systems have different file naming conventions, and therefore different ways of specifying a filename.

ISO-Pascal, the most widely used international standard, does not specify how filenames are to be associated. A widely used convention is the "ASSIGN" statement. This has the form:

```
ASSIGN( <file variable>,<filename>);
```

The <filename> is a literal string or a string variable. For example

```
ASSIGN( data_file, 'MY_DATA.DAT');
```

might be used with the MS-DOS system.

The ANSI standard for the C language combines stages 2 and 3 into one statement.

## Opening files

All operating systems employ the concept of open and closed files. There is an analogy with paper files. The computers backing store can be thought of as a filing cabinet. It may contain perhaps hundreds, or thousands of files. The files not currently in use are said to be closed, these are the ones in the cabinet. At any one time only a small number are being used, these are the ones on the desk. The action of finding a file in the cabinet and putting it on the desk is similar to the operating system opening a file. The operating system cannot read or write closed files.

To open a file in C the library routine called fopen is used. It takes two parameters, the first is the filename, the second is the access mode. The value returned is assigned to the file variable. The access mode determines whether data is to be read or written, and also distinguishes between text and binary mode. The following opens a file called 'my_data' for reading in text mode:

data_file = fopen("my_data","rt");

The modes available depend on the operating system, check with your compiler documentation.

To open a file in Pascal one of two commands are used, either RESET or REWRITE. RESET is used for reading from a file, and REWRITE is used for writing to a file. The file variable is given as a parameter. The following statements open "in_file" for reading and "out_file" for writing:

RESET( in_file);
REWRITE( out_file );

(Note: UCSD Pascal does not have an ASSIGN statement. The filename is given in the RESET REWRITE statements.)

To open a file in read mode it must already exist, but a file opened in write mode is created if it does not exist. If it does already exist it is deleted then re-created.

## Transferring data to and from files

For each file, the operating system maintains

a pointer which holds the position in the file of the next item to be read. When data is read from a file the pointer steps on one to the next item. Thus successive reads from the file return the items sequentially. Figure 10.2 illustrates this.

Each time an item of data is written to the file it is appended after the last item. Thus the length of the file grows with each item written. Both reading and writing are one directional processes, from the start of the file towards the end.

The mechanism to transfer data to or from a file is similar to that for communicating with a user via the keyboard or screen. The only difference is that a file variable is used to denote the destination or source of the data. Both C and Pascal use commands for file input very similar to those for user input. In

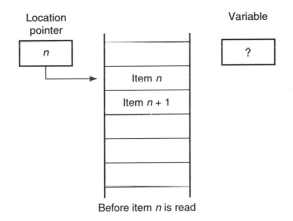

*Before item n is read*

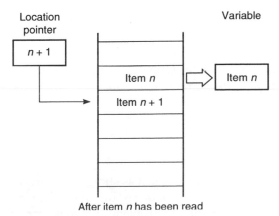

*After item n has been read*

**Figure 10.2** Reading items sequentially from a file.

Pascal these are READ and READLN, the only difference being that the first parameter must be the file variable. For example

```
READ(in_file, first_number,
second_number);
```

or

```
READLN(text_in, item, cost);
```

READ may be used with binary or text files, but READLN can only be used with text files.

For binary files the data type of the variables in the READ statement must be the same as the type in the declaration of the file variable. That is, if the file variable is declared as FILE OF REAL, then the variables must be of type REAL. This is checked at compile time and will cause a syntax error if incorrect.

For text files the system tries to interpret the next item in the file according to the data type of the corresponding variable. As the compiler cannot know the contents of the file, this check is performed at run-time. A run-time error will result if, for example, an alphabetic character is encountered when a numeric value is expected.

C uses the function fscanf, for file scanf, to read from files. This works exactly the same as scanf, the only difference being the first parameter is the file variable. For example

```
fscanf( in_file, "%s %e",  item,
cost);
```

The C compiler does not attempt to match file types and variable types. For binary files the incoming binary data is simply stored in the appropriate variable. If the file was not created using the same data types then the result will be indeterminate. Text files are treated similarly to Pascal the conversion from ASCII to binary may cause a run-time error if data of incorrect format is encountered.

Writing to a file is just as straightforward as reading. As the data in the file is being created there are no problems due to incorrect format.

Pascal uses WRITE or WRITELN , C uses fprintf. The first parameter in each case must be the file variable.

```
WRITE(out_file, temperature,
pressure);
WRITELN(text_out, 'The values are
:',angle,sine,cosine);
fprintf(out_file,"%f %f",
temperature,pressure);
fprintf(text_out,"The values
are:%d %f %f",angle,sine,cosine);
```

Figures 10.3 and 10.4 show programs for reading ten numbers from a binary file, displaying the numbers and the average.

```
#include <stdio.h>
FILE *in_file;
int i;
float number,
sum;
main()
{
in_file = fopen("numbers","rb");
sum = 0;
for ( i=1; i<11; i++) {
  fscanf(in_file,"%e", number);
  printf("Number %d is
  %e\n",i,number);
  sum = sum + number;
}
printf("The average is
%e\n",sum/10);
}
```

**Figure 10.3** An example of reading from a file.

```
PROGRAM File_average;
VAR in_file : FILE OF REAL;
i : INTEGER;
number,
sum : REAL;
BEGIN
  ASSIGN(in_file, 'numbers');
  RESET(in_file);
  sum := 0;
  FOR i := 1 TO 10 DO
  BEGIN
    READ(in_file,number);
    WRITELN('Number ',i,' is ',
    number);
    sum := sum + number;
  END
  WRITELN('The average is
  ',sum/10);
END.
```

**Figure 10.4** An example of reading from a file.

## DETECTING THE END OF A FILE

When reading data from a file a program must be able to determine when the last item has been read. Attempting to read past the end of a file will cause a run-time error. Languages which support file handling always have some means of detecting this condition.

Pascal has the function EOF which returns a boolean TRUE or FALSE, it takes the file variable as a parameter. In C the `feof` function performs the same role. End of file is often used as the continuation condition for a loop. For example

```
WHILE NOT EOF(a_file) DO
BEGIN
  .
  .
END;
while ( ! foef(a_file)) {
  .
  .
  .
}
```

## USING FILES AS A MEANS OF COMMUNICATION

As well as using files as a means of storage, they can be used to communicate data from one program to another. A program could be used to process some data and produce intermediate results. These results are written to a file. The file can then be transferred to a different computer and another program can be used to read the data and complete the processing. It is usual, under these circumstances, to employ text rather than binary files. The format of the file is easier to document, and the contents can be checked with an ordinary text editor.

A particularly powerful use of this technique is where data are transferred to, or from, a commercially available package, e.g. a database or spreadsheet. Consider a situation where some data have been collected and need processing before being presented in the form of graphs. A program could be written to read in and process the data. However, presenting the information graphically is a complex programming task. If the data are written to a file in the correct format they can be imported into a spreadsheet package with the necessary graphing capabilities. It is a wasteful use of programmers' time producing a graphics program when the facility is already available.

## SUMMARY

❏ Files can be used to provide input data to a program, or to receive output data from a program.

❏ Files can be used for storage of data, or for communication between programs.

❏ All references to a file within a program are by the file variable.

❏ Input and output to files is programmed similarly to input and output from keyboard and screen.

## EXERCISES

1. Write two programs to calculate the combined resistance of pairs of resistors in parallel. The first program is to read data from the keyboard and write it to a file. The data represents the values of pairs of resistors. The user must be able to control the number of pairs (i.e. the length of the file is not fixed).

   The second program must display one combined resistance value for each pair stored in the file.

   Note: the combined resistance of two resistors $R_1$ and $R_2$ is given by the formula:

$$R_p = \frac{R_1 \times R_2}{R_1 + R_2}.$$

2. Write a program to read a text file and display the contents with line numbers.
3. Write a program to read two numbers representing the upper and lower bounds of the value of $x$ in the following equation:

$$y = 3x^2 + 4x - 9$$

   The program must write data to a file in a suitable format for importing into a spreadsheet. The data represent values of $x$ and $y$ at sufficient points for a graph of the equation to be produced.
4. Why should the end of file condition be used in a pre-condition loop rather than a post-condition loop?

# Further programming techniques

## ARRAYS

Simple variables, sometimes called scalar data types, can only hold one item of data. Arrays are collections of data items, all with the same data type. If, for example, we are required to hold the rainfall for each month in a year, we could declare twelve variables called January, February, March, etc. A more satisfactory solution would be to declare an array called Months with twelve elements.

A variable can be envisaged as a box in which to put data. An array, therefore is a pile of boxes all holding similar data. Each box has a number or index. A program can only access one box at a time, but the box can be chosen at run time.

The data required to store the exam results for a class of twelve students is shown in Figs 11.1 and 11.2. The amount of storage space is

the same, but the program has much more flexible access to the data in the array.

### Declaring arrays

When an array is declared the compiler must know how much memory the array will require. An array declaration in C follows the identifier with the number of elements in square brackets.

```
int exam_marks[12];
```

Arrays in C all start from element zero so the elements will be numbered 0–11.

Pascal uses the keyword ARRAY to denote an array data type:

```
VAR exam_mark:ARRAY[1..12] OF
INTEGER;
```

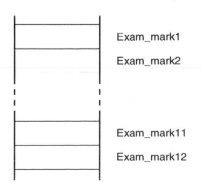

**Figure 11.1** The memory requirements for twelve separate variables.

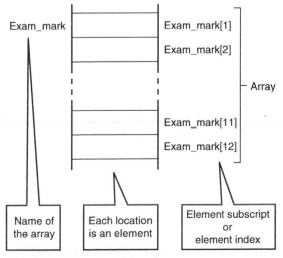

**Figure 11.2** The structure of an array.

The range in the square brackets denotes the first and last element numbers.

### Accessing array elements

An array element may be used anywhere in a program where a simple variable of the same data type can be used. The array name is followed by the element index in square brackets. The index is calculated at run time, and must be an expression which returns an integer value. Pascal incorporates run-time checks to ensure the index does not go out of range, C does not perform any checks on the array index, this often causes problems for novice programmers!

In Fig. 11.3 the for loop causes the process of prompting for and reading a student's mark to be repeated twelve times. The first time through the loop the data is entered into the first element of the array (element 0 for C, element 1 for Pascal). This process is repeated, with each successive time through the loop reading data into the next element in the array. If simple variables had been used then twelve input and twelve output statements would have been needed.

The above examples show arrays of integers, but any data type can be used, including arrays of arrays!

# STRUCTURED DATA TYPES

We have used simple data types for single items of data, and arrays for many items of the same type. These two cover most data storage situations, but there are occasions when we wish to refer to items of a different type as one unit.

For example, suppose we require a program to process weather information. We want to store the name of ten cities and, for each city, the annual rainfall (in millimetres) and the average temperature. We could use three arrays. An array of strings for the name, an array of integers for the rainfall, and an array of floating point numbers for the average temperature. This approach separates the three items, what we need is to be able to

```
FOR i : = 1 TO 12 DO
BEGIN
    WRITELN("Please   enter   the
mark    for student" , i);
    READLN( exam _mark [i]);
END;
for ( i=0 ; i < 12; i ++ ) {
    printf("Please enter the
    mark for student %d",i);
    scanf ("%d",&exam_mark[i]);
    }
```

**Figure 11.3** Reading twelve exam marks into an array.

group the three items of data into one entity. For this we use a structured data type.

Structured data types consist of a number of data items, which need not be of the same type, grouped together. The structured type can be treated as a single entity, or the individual item may be accessed separately.

Pascal calls structured types RECORDs, with the individual items known as fields. In C they are called structs, and the individual items are members.

### Declaring a structured type

A RECORD declaration in Pascal looks like:

```
VAR city :RECORD
        name          :STRING[20];
        rainfall    :INTEGER;
        temperature :REAL;
END;
```

The keyword RECORD shows the start of the structure, followed by the field declarations, and completed with END. This will only declare one record for one city. To declare an array we could use

```
VAR  cities :ARRAY[1 . . . 10]
OF RECORD
    name          :STRING[20];
    rainfall    :INTEGER;
    temperature :REAL;
    END;
```

but this is rather cumbersome. A better technique is to define the record as a new type. User-defined types are declared thus:

```
TYPE  city_data = RECORD
           name          :STRING[20];
           rainfall      :INTEGER;
           temperature   :REAL;
     END;
```

The actual array is then declared:

```
VAR   cities:ARRAY[1..10] OF
city_data;
```

Declaring a `struct` in C is similar

```
struct    city_data {
          char   name[20];
          int    rainfall;
          float  temperature;
          } city;
```

This defines a new structured type called city_data, and one data item of this type called city. A more usual method is to define the type and declare the data separately

```
struct   city_data {
         char   name[20];
         int    rainfall;
         float temperature;
         };
struct   city_data cities[10];
```

## Accessing members and fields of structured types

Access to the individual items of a structured type is provided by the dot notation. The member, or field, name is appended to the variable name separated by a dot. So to set the rainfall of the city variable to 100 we would use

```
Pascal
city.rainfall := 100;
```

```
C
city.rainfall = 100;
```

When a structured type is an element in an array, then the array index comes before the

dot. To display the value of the average temperature for the fourth city we might use:

```
Pascal
WRITELN(cities[4].temperature);
```

```
C
printf("%f",cities[3].
temperature);
```

## LOCAL VARIABLES

All the variables we have used so far have what is called global scope. A variable with global scope may be referenced from anywhere in the program. For a variable to have global scope it must be declared outside of any procedure or function, usually at the start of the program. Sometimes it is convenient to restrict access to a variable to just one module. To do this the variable is declared with local scope. A variable declared inside a module has its scope restricted to just that module. A local variable does not exist outside of the block in which it is declared. Use of local variables is helpful in increasing the independence of modules, which is desirable for maintenance and portability reasons. Figure 11.4 shows some declarations of local variables.

As well as its scope, a variable has a lifetime. The lifetime of a variable is how long

```
PROCEDURE  Local_vars;
VAR  one, two,three:INTEGER;
BEGIN
   .
   .

   .
END;
local_vars()
{
int one,two,three;
   .

   .
   .

}
```

**Figure 11.4** Local variable declarations.

a value is retained in the variable. Global variables have program lifetime, the value is retained as long as the program is running. Local variables only have module lifetime. When the module exits, and control returns to the calling module, the value of any local variable are discarded. Thus values of local variables are not retained between calls.

# PASSING DATA TO OR FROM MODULES

The procedures (and C functions) we have met so far have not been very flexible. Each time they are called they perform their operations on the same data variables and return the result in the same variables. This is rather like a bus which travels a fixed route. A taxi on the other hand will go to a different destination each time it is used depending on instructions given to it at the time. It would be useful if we could have a more general module which could be given different data to use each time it is called. The module would always perform the same operations but each time with different data. This is achieved with use of parameters, sometimes called arguments in C.

In fact we have already met parameters. The items in the brackets after READLN, scanf, WRITELN and printf are parameters (arguments). The information we require to be displayed on the screen is passed to printf or WRITELN as parameters. The parameters control the actions taken by the output routines.

We indicate that a module has parameters when it is declared. The identifier is followed by a parameter list in round brackets. These are known as the formal parameters. Each parameter has an associated data type. Figure 11.5 shows examples of declarations in C and Pascal.

When the procedure, or function, is called the identifier is followed by an actual parameter list in round brackets. This data is passed to the module and can be referenced inside the module by the formal parameter names. There are two mechanisms for passing data via parameters:

- Passing by value
- Passing by reference.

### Passing by value

This type of parameter is used only to pass data into the module. The actual parameter is not changed by the execution of the module.

Value parameters may be a

- constant
- variable
- expression

of the same type as the formal parameter.

Local data space is allocated by the compiler for each value parameter. At the module call the value of each actual parameter is copied into the corresponding formal parameter. Within the module reference to the formal parameter will refer to this copy, thus any changes made will only change the copy, not the original actual parameter. This process is illustrated in Fig. 11.6.

```
line_of_stars(int stars)
box(int height, width)
power_of(float number; int index)

PROCEDURE    line_of_stars(stars:INTEGER);
PROCEDURE    box(height, width:INTEGER);
PROCEDURE    power_of(number:REAL; index:INTEGER);
```

**Figure 11.5** Examples of declaration with formal parameters.

## Passing by reference

The only actual parameters that can be passed by reference are variables. The module declaration indicates whether or not a variable is to be passed by reference. In C an asterisk is used to denote a pointer to the variable required. For example

```
double( int *value)
swap( int * first, *second)
```

Pascal uses the keyword VAR to indicate passing by reference.

```
PROCEDURE double (VAR value:
INTEGER);
PROCEDURE swap (VAR first,
second:INTEGER);
```

When a parameter is passed by reference any changes made to the formal parameter will also change the actual parameter. By this mechanism data can be passed both into and out of the called module. Figure 11.7 illustrates the process of passing by reference.

With Pascal the only requirement to use parameters by reference is to insert the keyword VAR in the declaration, but with C there are several other points to take into account. The variable names in the actual parameter list must be preceded by an ampersand (&), this informs the compiler that a reference (pointer) to the variable must be passed, and not a copy. Also references to the actual parameters within the function must have an asterisk prepended to indicate that this is a pointer not a value. Figure 11.8 shows an example of passing by reference and value.

## TYPED FUNCTIONS

A typed function is similar to an ordinary function or procedure except that it has a value. A typed function returns a value wherever it is called. Typed functions may be used anywhere an expression can be used. The principle use of typed functions is to calculate a value based upon data given to it as a parameter. The type of function can be any basic type or user defined type. Consider a situation where we wish to calculate the factorial of some numbers. We could write a module to do the calculations and put the answer in a global variable (or we could use a reference parameter). But a typed function is a neater solution, see Fig. 11.9.

We can see that there are two differences between a typed function and an ordinary procedure or function. The first is the declaration. Pascal uses the keyword FUNCTION instead of PROCEDURE, and the type of the function follows the declaration. The declaration of a typed function in C only entails preceding the function name with its type. The other difference is shown by the last but one line in each of the functions in Fig. 11.9. This is the return mechanism. For Pascal the value to be returned is assigned to the function name. In C the keyword return is used followed by an expression, it is convention to enclose this in parentheses.

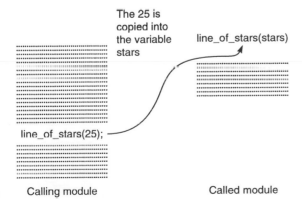

**Figure 11.6** Passing by value.

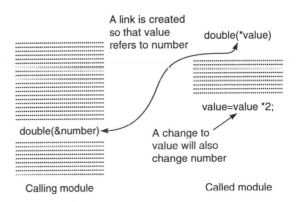

**Figure 11.7** Passing by reference.

```
PROGRAM  Time_gone(INPUT,OUTPUT);
  VAR    minutes,
         time_hours,
         time_minutes    :INTEGER;
         afternoon        :BOOLEAN;

  PROCEDURE  Minutes_since_midnight(minutes_gone:      INTEGER);

  VAR    hours,
         minutes          :INTEGER;
  VAR    pm   :BOOLEAN);

  BEGIN
         hours := minutes_gone DIV 60;
         minutes := minutes_gone MOD 60;
         IF hours > 12 THEN
         BEGIN
             hours := hours - 12;
             pm := TRUE;
      END
      ELSE pm := FALSE;
  END;

BEGIN
  WRITELN('Enter the number of minutes since midnight');
  READLN (minutes);
  Minutes_since_midnight(minutes,time_hours,time_minutes,afternoon)
  WRITE(' Time is :,time_hours:2,':',time_minutes:2);
  IF afternoon  THEN WRITELN(' PM')
                ELSE WRITELN(' AM');
END.
}
```

**Figure 11.8**  (continues on page 101).

```
#include < stdio.h>

minutes_since_midnight( int minutes_gone;
                        int *hours,
                             *minutes,
                             *pm)

  {
    *hours = minutes_gone / 60;
    *minutes = minutes_gone % 60;
    if (*hours > 12) {
        *hours = *hours - 12;
        *pm = 1;
  }
  else *pm = 0;

main()
{
  int    minutes,
         time_minutes,
         time_hours,
         afternoon;
  printf("Enter the number of minutes since midnight");
  scanf (&minutes);
  minutes_since_midnight(minutes,&time_hours,&time_minutes,&after
  noon);
  printf("Time is:%2d:%2d"',time_hours,time_minutes);
  if (afternoon)  printf(" PM\n");
    else  printf(" AM\n");
  }
```

**Figure 11.8** Using parameters.

```
  int  factorial (int value)
  {
  int fact;
  fact = 1;
  for ( ; value != 0; value--)
    fact = fact * value;
  return (fact);
  }
FUNCTION Factorial (value:INTEGER):INTEGER;
VAR fact:INTEGER;
BEGIN
  fact := 1;
  FOR value := value DOWNTO 1 DO
    fact := fact * value;
  Factorial := fact;
END;
```

**Figure 11.9** Typed functions to return a factorial.

# LIBRARY FUNCTIONS

Most language systems provide a library of frequently used functions these include mathematical and other operations. Some of those usually available are:

|                 | C                  | Pascal   |
|-----------------|--------------------|----------|
| Sine            | sin(x)             | Sin(x)   |
| Cosine          | cos(x)             | Cos(x)   |
| Logarithm       | log(x)             | Ln(x)    |
| Arc tangent     | atan(x)            | Atan(x)  |
| Square root     | sqrt(x)            | Sqrt(x)  |
| Rounding        | ceil(x), floor(x)  | Round(x) |
| Random number   | rand(x)            | Rand(x)  |

A language implementation may provide many more library functions of a specialist nature for graphics, sound, etc.

# EXERCISES

1. Design and write a program to accept a list of positive numbers ending with a zero. The program must display the average of all the numbers (not including the zero), and also how many numbers exceeded the average and how may were less than the average.

2. Design and write a program which reads up to twenty student names and their exam marks from the keyboard. The program must then list the students in order of their success in the exam. (Hint: research some standard sort algorithms.)

3. Each entry in a stock control system is represented by:

   ■ A part number
   ■ A descriptive name
   ■ The current stock level
   ■ The minimum stock level
   ■ The cost per item.

   Define a structured data type to hold this information.

   Write a simple program to read the details of several stock items and display them.

4. Define a structured data type to hold a date as day, month and year numerically.

   Add two members (fields) to the structure in Exercise 3 above:

   ■ The date of the last delivery,
   ■ The date of the last order.

5. Write a function to return the cube of a number.

# Appendix A: Assignments

Two assignments are given here: one with a solution and one for the reader to attempt.

## ASSIGNMENT 1: WORKED ASSIGNMENT

### Task

Produce a design and a working program in your chosen language for the following.

### Specification

A program is required to process numerical data which is held in blocks.

The first number in each block is a length indicator which gives the number of data items in the block. The indicator is not part of the data.

For example, a typical block could consist of:

3   12   –34   56

where 3 is the block length indicator indicating three numbers in the block and 12, –34 and 56 are the numbers to be processed.

Data processing is terminated when a block length indicator of zero is read. Thus a typical set of data could be:

```
2   3    4
4   –6   56   78   –1
7   14   128  –86  3   42   0   71
0
```

For each block, the program must determine and display to the screen:

- the count of the positive numbers
- the count of the negative numbers
- the average
- the numerical range.

### Solution

*Program operation.* The program continually processes the numerical blocks until a block indicator of zero is input.

The processing of each block consists of:

- Initialize the counts; block sum, positive numbers, negative numbers
- Process each number in the block, one at a time
- Output the required data.

The processing for each number in the block consists of:

- Request input of the next number
- Add the number to the sum
- Determine the sign and increment the appropriate count
- Determine if this number is higher or lower than the current highest and lowest. If so adjust as appropriate. (The first number in the block is both highest and lowest.)

*Limitations.* There is no data validation of the input.

## Pseudocode

```
Input block indicator
  Output blank line
  Output operator prompt
  Read block length indicator

Loop while block indicator not 0
  Process block

    Initialize block
      Zero sum
      Zero positive count
      Zero negative count

    Process block numbers
      Loop for block length times
        Output operator prompt
        Read next data item
        Add item to sum
        Determine sign of item
          if item < 0
          then
            increment negative count
          else
            increment positive count
          endif
        Determine range
          if first number in block
          then
            highest = item
            lowest = item
          else
            if item > highest
            then
              highest = item
            else
              if item < lowest
            then
              lowest = item
              endif
            endif
          endif
      end loop
    Output block data
      Output header data
      Output positive count
      Output negative count
      Calculate and output average
```

```
      Output numerical range
    Input block length indicator
      Output blank line
      Output operator prompt
      Read block indicator
end loop
```

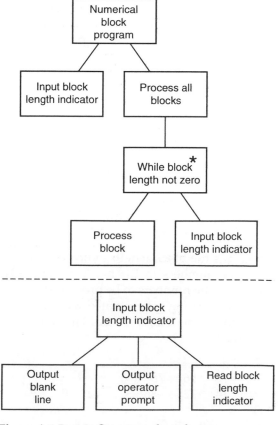

**Figure A.1 Part 1**  Structure chart design.

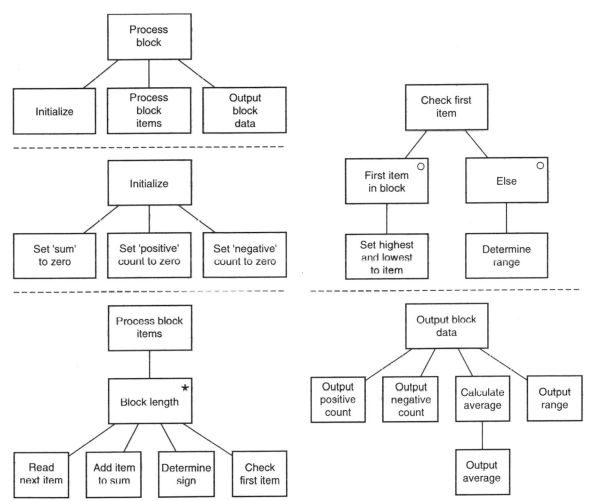

**Figure A.1 Part 2** Structure chart design.

**Figure A.1 Part 3** Structure chart design.

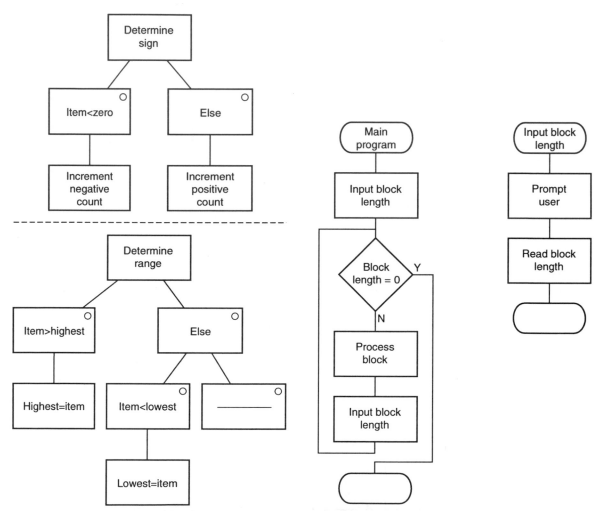

**Figure A.1 Part 4** Structure chart design.

**Figure A.2 Part 1** Flowchart design.

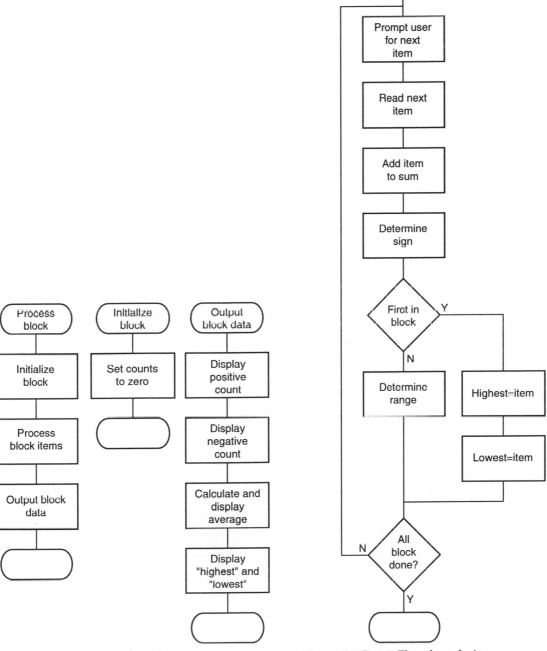

**Figure A.2 Part 2** Flowchart design.

**Figure A.2 Part 3** Flowchart design.

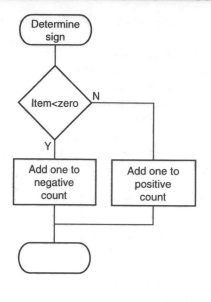

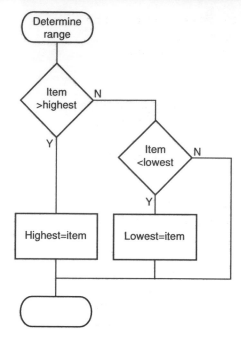

**Figure A.2 Part 4** Flowchart design.

```
{********************************
Program name:        Appendix_A
 File name: APPNDX_A.PAS
 Author:      A. N. Other
 Origination date:        Dec 1993
 Language:  Turbo Pascal V6
```

This program processes numerical data which is held in blocks.

The first number in each block is a length indicator which gives the number of data items in the block. The indicator is not part of the data.

Data processing is terminated when a block length indicator of zero is read.

For each block, the program must determine and display to the screen:

■ the count of the positive numbers

■ the count of the negative numbers
■ the average
■ the numerical range

```
********************************}

PROGRAM Process_blocks (INPUT,OUT-
PUT);

VAR
  block_length,
  block_item,
  highest_number,
  lowest_number,
  negative_count,
  positive_count,
  sum  :INTEGER;

{****INPUT BLOCK LENGTH VALUE*****
Prompt the operator for the next
block length and read it into
'block_length'
 }
PROCEDURE Input_block_length;
  BEGIN
    WRITELN;
```

```
    WRITE('Please enter the next
block indicator : ');
    READLN(block_length);
  END;


{******** INITIALIZE BLOCK********
Set the block counts to zero
 }
PROCEDURE Initialize_block;
  BEGIN
    sum := 0;
    positive_count := 0;
    negative_count := 0;
  END;


{*********DETERMINE SIGN**********
Determine whether the number is
positive or negative, and incre-
ment the appropriate count.
 }
PROCEDURE Determine_sign;
  BEGIN
    IF block_item < 0
    THEN
      negative_count :=
negative_count + 1
    ELSE
      positive_count :=
positive_count + 1;
  END;


{********DETERMINE RANGE**********
Determine if the current item
increases the numerical range, and
adjust the highest or lowest value
if required
 }
PROCEDURE Determine_range;
  BEGIN
    IF block_item > highest_number
    THEN
      highest_number := block_item
    ELSE
      IF block_item < lowest_number
      THEN
        lowest_number :=
block_item;
  END;
```

```
{******PROCESS BLOCK ITEMS********
Process each number in the block.
For each number:
■ add it to the sum
■ determine the sign
■ determine the range
 }
PROCEDURE Process_block_items;
  VAR i : INTEGER; { Local FOR
loop counter }
  BEGIN
    FOR i := 1 TO block_length DO
    BEGIN
      WRITELN;
      WRITE('Please input the next
item : ');
      READ(block_item);
      sum := sum + block_item;
      Determine_sign;
      IF i = 1 THEN
      BEGIN
        highest_number :=
block_item;
        lowest_number :=
block_item;
      END
      ELSE
        Determine_range;
    END
  END;


{******OUTPUT BLOCK DATA *********
Output the required data for this
block
}
PROCEDURE Output_block_data;
  BEGIN
    WRITELN;
    WRITELN('****************');
    WRITELN;
    WRITELN('The count of positive
numbers is: ',positive_count);
    WRITELN;
    WRITELN('The count of negative
numbers is: ',negative_count);
    WRITELN;
    WRITELN('The average of the
block items is:
',(sum/block_length):6:2);
```

```
    WRITELN;
    WRITELN('The numerical range
is from ',lowest_number,'
to',highest_number);
  END;
{********PROCESS BLOCK **********
Process one whole block
 }
PROCEDURE Process_block;
  BEGIN
    Initialize_block;
    Process_block_items;
    Output_block_data;
  END;

{*************MAIN BODY ***********
Process each block until the block
length indicator is zero
 }
BEGIN
  Input_block_length;
  WHILE block_length <> 0 DO
  BEGIN
    Process_block;
    Input_block_length;
  END;
END.
{*******************************}


/*******************************
  Program name:    Appendix_A
  File name:       APPNDX_A.C
  Author:          A. N. Other
  Origiation date: Dec 1993
  Language:        TopSpeed C V3.2
```

This program processes
numerical data which is held in
blocks.

The first number in each block is a
length indicator which gives the
number of data items in the block.
The indicator is not part of the
data.

Data processing is terminated when
a block length indicator of zero
is read.

For each block, the program must
determine and display to the
screen:

■ the count of the positive
  numbers
■ the count of the negative
  numbers
■ the average
■ the numerical range

```
*********************************/

  #include <stdio.h>

  int
    block_length,
    block_item,
    highest_number,
    lowest_number,
    negative_count,
    positive_count,
    sum;

float  block_average;

/*** INPUT BLOCK LENGTH VALUE ****
Prompt the operator for the next
block length and read it into
'block_length'*/

  input_block_length()
  {
   printf("\nPlease enter the
   next block indicator : ");
   scanf("%d",&block_length);
  }

/******** INITIALISE BLOCK *******
Set the block counts to zero
*/

initialise_block()

    {
    sum = 0;
    positive_count = 0;
    negative_count = 0;
    }
```

```
/******** DETERMINE SIGN *********
Determine whether the number is
positive or negative, and
increment the appropriate count.
*/

  determine_sign()

   {
    if ( block_item < 0 )
    negative_count++;
    else  positive_count++;
    }

/******* DETERMINE RANGE *********
Determine if the current item
increases the numerical range,
and adjust the highest or lowest
value if required
*/

  determine_range()

     {
      if ( block_item >
     highest_number)
       highest_number =
       block_item;
       else
       if ( block_item <
       lowest_number)
       lowest_number = block_item;
    }


/****** PROCESS BLOCK ITEMS ******
Process each number in the block.
For each number:
```

- add it to the sum
- determine the sign
- determine the range
```
*/

    process_block_items()

    {
    int  i;  /* Local 'for' loop
    counter */
```

```
    for  (i = 1; i <=
    block_length; i++)
    {
      printf("\nPlease input the
      next item : ");
      scanf("%d",&block_item);

      sum = sum + block_item;

      determine_sign();
      if (1 == i )
      {
      highest_number =
      block_item;
        lowest_number  =
        block_item;
        }
        else
          determine_range();
      }
    }


/******* OUTPUT BLOCK DATA *******
Output the required data for this
block
*/

    output_block_data()

    {
printf("\n******************\n");
      printf("\nThe count of
      positive numbers is:
      %d\n",positive_count);
      printf("\nThe count of
      negative numbers is:
      %d\n",negative_count);
      block_average = (float) sum /
      block_length;
      printf("\nThe average of the
      block items is:
      %6.2f\n",block_average);
      printf("\nThe numerical range
      is from %d to
      %d\n",lowest_number,highest_n
      umber);
      }
```

```
/******** PROCESS BLOCK **********
   Process one whole block
   */

  process_block()

  {
    initialise_block();
    process_block_items();
    output_block_data();
  }

/*********** MAIN BODY ***********
   Process each block until the
   block length indicator is zero
   */
   main()
   {
     input_block_length();

     while ( block_length != 0)
     {
       process_block();
       input_block_length();
     }
   }

/*******************************/
```

The length of the beam ($L$) and the load ($F$) is to specified by the user when the program is run.

For the specified beam length and point load, the program is to generate a table of beam reactions at points $R_1$ and $R_2$ when the load is placed at the eleven positions equi-spaced as indicated in Fig. A.3. The formulae required are given in Fig. A.4.

If required, the program should also indicate the beam reactions when the point load is positioned at any user specified position, which may be different from the eleven positions in Fig. A.4.

The program should offer the user another run if required.

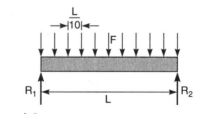

**Figure A.3**

# ASSIGNMENT 2

Design and produce a program complete with documentation to meet the scenario detailed below.

## Scenario

As a trainee software engineer in your company, you have been given the task to provide a computer program for use by civil engineers.

The program is to be used to calculate the loading on a beam by a single point load which can be positioned at any point along the length of the beam.

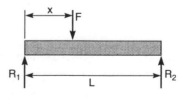

$$R_1 = \frac{F}{L}(L-x), \qquad R_2 = \frac{F}{L}x$$

**Figure A.4**

# Appendix B: Reserved words in C and Pascal

Reserved words cannot be used as identifiers. The following are reserved words for C and Pascal.

## Reserved words in C

| | | |
|---|---|---|
| auto | extern | short |
| break | float | sizeof |
| case | for | static |
| char | goto | struct |
| continue | if | switch |
| default | int | typedef |
| do | long | union |
| double | register | unsigned |
| else | return | while |

## Reserved words in Pascal

| | | | |
|---|---|---|---|
| AND | END | NOT | THEN |
| ARRAY | FILE | OF | TO |
| BEGIN | FOR | OR | TYPE |
| CASE | FUNCTION | PACKED | UNTIL |
| CONST | GOTO | PROCEDURE | VAR |
| DIV | IF | PROGRAM | WHILE |
| DO | IN | RECORD | WITH |
| DOWNTO | MOD | REPEAT | |
| ELSE | NIL | STRING | |

The following are required words. They may be used as identifiers, though this is not recommended.

| | |
|---|---|
| BOOLEAN | READ |
| CHAR | READLN |
| INPUT | WRITE |
| INTEGER | WRITELN |
| OUTPUT | |

# Index